Contemporary Crafts

Pottery
and
Ceramics

LIZA GARDNER

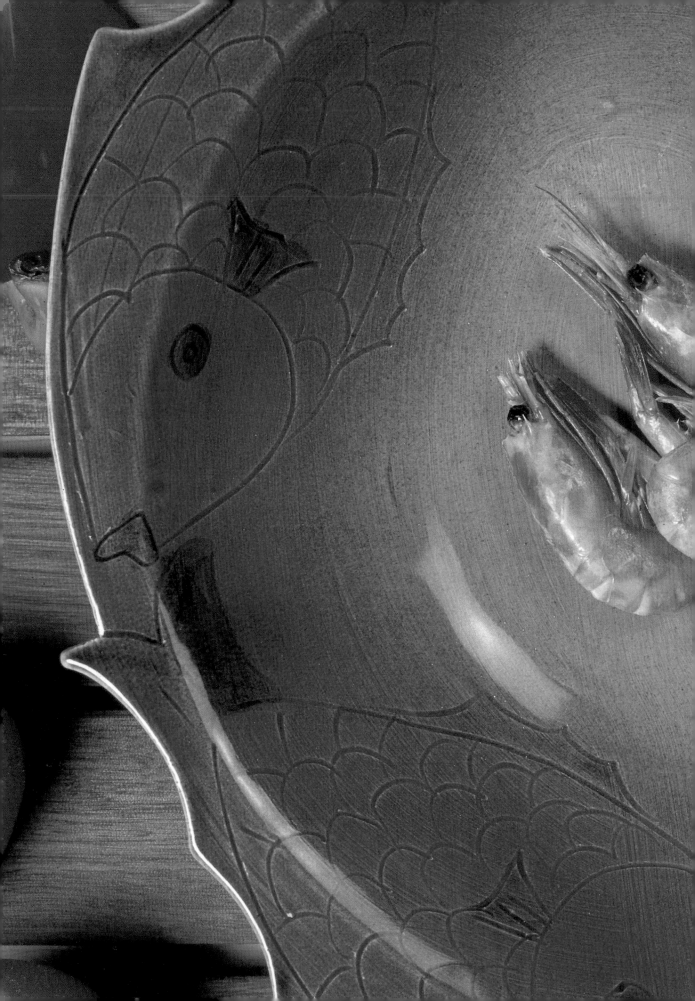

Contemporary Crafts

Pottery
and
Ceramics

Liza Gardner

NEW
HOLLAND

Dedicated to my children, Chloe, whose work appears on page 78 and my son, Orlando Delacroix, who, at six months old, is still a little small to have discovered clay.

This edition published in 1998 by
New Holland Publishers (UK) Ltd
London • Cape Town • Sydney • Auckland

24 Nutford Place
London W1H 6DQ
United Kingdom

80 McKenzie Street
Cape Town 8001
South Africa

3/2 Aquatic Drive
Frenchs Forest
NSW 2086
Australia

Unit 1A, 218 Lake Road
Northcote
Auckland
New Zealand

ISBN 1 85368 868 1

Managing Editor: Coral Walker
Designer: Paul Cooper
Photographer: Shona Wood

Acknowledgements
Thanks to Tony Southgate and Harry Frazier from Potclays for the kind loan of the kiln on page 10. Pam Smith of Pottery Crafts for the loan of the majority of the tools featured on pages 12-15. Paul Crick from Specialist Crafts Ltd for the loan of the banding wheel used throughout the book, the hobby spray gun, brush-on glazes and also the ceramic paints used in Painted Plate project on page 50. Craig Peebles of W J Furse & Co Ltd (Pumps) for the very kind gift of the small pump used in the Wall Fountain project on page 82. And finally, Sam Faraway, my ex-apprentice for his extraordinary help and patience.

Reproduction by P & W Graphics
Printed and bound in Singapore by Tien Wah Press (Pte) Ltd

6 8 10 9 7

CONTENTS

INTRODUCTION

AN INTRODUCTION TO an art form as wide and ancient as that of ceramics needs far more pages than I have at my disposal; I can only provide a token selection from the many historical landmarks of style and innovation. However, I would also like to explain how I came to work in this medium, the enthusiasm that keeps me working and, hopefully, impart some of my passion for clay to you. For those who may wish to explore the diverse history of ceramics in greater detail, I have provided a short, further reading list on page 95.

One of the great bonuses of being asked to write a book such as this, is that it becomes a necessity to find the time to research all the work that you really love. If you have the time, I recommend it. Take a sketch book or a camera to record what you like: sometimes just a tiny detail executed in a different medium or discipline, such as silverware or furniture can inspire you, leading you on to a fresh new idea that can be later executed in clay.

When I was aged 12 or so, I discovered how remarkably easy it is to model clay into simple shapes such as animals. A hedgehog was one of my early successes. He was such a simple form - just a hollow egg shape with a pinched nose, two dots for eyes and some scratches on his back for the spines. A year or two later, I was

This exquisite French dish in the style of Bernard Palissy dates to the mid-18th century. It is made from earthenware and decorated with lead glazes.

. . . .

privileged to help in the reconstruction of a medieval pottery located in an open air museum, building kilns and pottery machinery based on authentic medieval designs. A great number of people – both professional and amateur – were involved in the pottery and the feeling of camaraderie that was engendered was something I have never forgotten.

While working at the museum, the hedgehog shape I had produced, metamorphosed into a small clay whistle called an ocarina. A potter employed by the museum cut a number of note holes across his back and formed a mouthpiece by cutting a small slit in the underside. You could play a tune by blowing through the nose and fingering the holes. A peculiar thing to make from clay, a musical instrument, but it opened my eyes further to the possibilities of the medium.

For real medieval pottery, it is well worth looking at Thomas Toft, a potter of such originality and skill that he was repeatedly commissioned to design various commemorative plates for 17th-century English royalty. What set Toft apart from his contemporaries was the skill with which he could manipulate a slip trailer, giving extremely fine lines of slip and very small dots or 'pearls'. Another factor was the size of his platters, the larger the plate – or 'charger' as they are correctly called – the more susceptible they are to warping or 'dunting' in the kiln. (Dunting is the term for a crack or split that appears in work when it is cooling in the kiln, usually due to cold air being introduced into the

This classic blue and white Jasper snake handled or 'Venus'
vase by Wedgwood dates to c1785.

. . . .

glazed earthenware with vivid colours that favoured greens, blues and yellows. The forms he would sprig were as varied as lizards, snakes, shells and foliage. On the whole, his work was inspired by the then current Italian fashion for fantastical grottoes. He was later employed by Catherine de Medici in 1566 who very kindly set him up in a workshop in Paris.

Perhaps a more well known example of sprigging is that of Joshia Wedgwood who, in conjunction with the modelling skills of the sculptors John Flaxman (both senior and junior), refined the technique in a hugely successful emulation of ancient Greek ceramic art.

Wedgwood was born in Staffordshire, England in 1730 and by the age of 14 was indentured to his older brother Thomas. Subsequently, he went into partnership with Thomas Whieldon, one of the acknowledged ceramic geniuses of his day. The partnership lasted for five years, after which Wedgwood set up his first solo venture in 1759.

The principal problem faced by manufacturers of ceramics in the 18th century was that of inconsistency in the colour of the glaze. A popular range of tableware of the time was generically known as Cream Ware. This was made with varying degrees of success by most of the Staffordshire potters. However, to obtain the even coating of glaze, free of errant specks of iron oxides or crazing that the consumer desired, was the passport to commercial supremacy.

The methodology Wedgwood employed in his experiments to solve this problem and his recording of the same, provide an understanding of the man's business priorities at an early stage of his redoubtable career. Firstly, all his experiments were meticulously recorded and numbered, a principle I strongly uphold. Secondly, he employed a code to protect his findings from being of any advantage to others. This principle however, I am less happy about. I feel personally that knowledge should be shared, passed on, enabling others in their turn to discover something new. In this book I hope you will learn some of things that I have discovered, from working with others or from

kiln too early or an incompatibility of glaze and body whereby the two components contract at different rates.) The slip trailing technique for which Toft is renowned is similar to that used in the Wisteria Platter project on page 88.

Another technique of some pedigree that I have used in this book is sprigging: placing small cast slabs of clay on to the main body of a vase or bowl. One of the prime influences for me very early on was the work of Bernard Palissy, born in France around 1510. His known and directly attributable work dates mainly from the latter half of the 16th century up to 1590 when he died.

Palissy made oval platters using both high- and low-relief sprigging techniques in lead

my own experiments. I hope you will take these ideas and improve on them!

Wedgwood's last ceramic invention was Jasper ware. A high-fired stoneware with a blue body and white sprigs placed on splendid forms.

Across the Atlantic, pottery was developing in a slightly different way. When the Spanish first landed in South America and looted their way to the Aztec capital in 1519 they purloined a rich haul of pottery as well as vast amounts of gold and silver. Fantastic vases and jugs with the heads of animals or deities modelled on the spouts were shipped back to Europe.

One main quality that differentiated this work from its European counterpart was the lack of glaze. Slip, or as it is sometimes known, engobe, was painted on to the dry body and then burnished. The burnishing was usually done with a small, smooth pebble rubbed rapidly over the pot when the slip had dried to give the piece an overall look of a smooth, polished stone. The pots would then be low-fired using wood and sawdust in an open pit. The low temperature used enabled the polished slip to retain its high sheen. This technique is still extensively used by the Pueblo Indians of New Mexico.

William de Morgan is another great favourite of mine although he was not, strictly speaking, a 'hands on' potter until later in his career. He was one of the most inventive designers working with ceramics as his chosen medium. Born in London in 1839, he studied fine art painting at the Royal Academy. After graduation he worked for William Morris, designing stained glass and tiles. Shortly after this, he set up his own design company and by the end of the 1860s had started to decorate the pottery himself.

Whilst running his own business, de Morgan became closely involved in the technical side of ceramics and was moved to experiment with lustre ware. He drew his influences from 15th-century southern Spain and Persian Islamic designs. Within these styles he became particularly well known for tiles and tile panels, a type of work which was soon taken up and copied by many of his contemporaries.

Around 1880, de Morgan moved his pottery to the site of Morris's Merton Abbey Mills, later becoming involved with the first Arts and Crafts Exhibition in 1888 in London.

Should you wish to follow the examples of any of the potters mentioned above, you will need to gain access to the various machinery required. It is worth considering enrolling in an evening class or perhaps finding a local potter who will let you work in his or her studio for a small hire fee. (This is something I have been happy to help with myself.) Many educational establishments will also have a kiln in which you can fire your work. If you enrol as a part time or a short course student, then having developed a rapport with the lecturer, you can avail yourself of the kiln whenever possible. Also enquire at local ceramic materials suppliers if they provide short courses. Many companies do as it is in their interest to introduce more people to ceramics.

This impressive tile panel of a 'lion rampant' by William de Morgan dates to c1887-1898.

. . . .

MATERIALS AND EQUIPMENT

All the materials and equipment shown in this chapter are of use to the ceramicist, but that is not to say that they are essential. A great many of the tools shown over the page can be improvised from discarded household items. An out-of-date credit card is a most useful smoothing tool, the wire bands from packing cases make serviceable turning tools, pencils, bits of old wood can all be shaped into the modelling tool that is perfect for the form you are about to make

However, at the risk of stating the obvious, some of the materials and equipment can be dangerous if used incorrectly or irresponsibly. For example, kilns get very hot; an over-enthusiastic look through the spy-hole when checking the progress of a firing can result in singed eyelashes at best. Many of the compounds used in glazes should never be ingested, hence the overriding necessity to use a good quality respirator whenever spraying or mixing glaze.

KILNS

A kiln represents a large investment for most people, even a fairly small model. Should you not wish to buy a kiln straight away, it is possible to borrow or rent space in someone else's kiln.

Having said that, the photograph on this page shows a natty little kiln which can be placed on a kitchen worktop and just plugged into the wall. It is small but would accommodate most work.

For more ambitious work, a larger kiln fitted

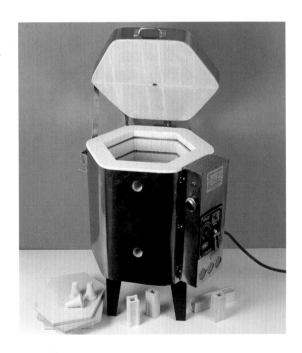

A small, tabletop kiln fitted with a basic 'kiln sitter' device that will automatically turn off the kiln when the required temperature is reached.

. . . .

with an electronic timer, which allows one to take advantage of cheap-time electricity, is a more expensive option.

Should you wish to buy your own kiln, you will need to purchase a set of kiln furniture. A

set comprises some shelves, either full or half width, props which enable one to vary the height of the shelves and plugs which are used to seal the spy holes while firing.

Small triangular stilts are used to raise the base of the glazed work from the kiln shelf when firing to prevent the molten glaze sticking to the shelf. Finally, some pyrometric cones can be of use if you do not have a reliable method of gauging the internal temperature of your kiln. Personally, I rarely use them, preferring a computer controlled temperature regulator. If you wish to buy a controller, do phone around for prices, as exactly the same controller can vary by a huge amount depending on which company's name is printed on the front panel.

I have only mentioned electric kilns, as all the projects in this book were fired using electricity, but natural gas, propane gas, oil and even wood burning kilns are all available.

WHEEL

The picture below shows a simple but serviceable electric wheel. Consider the ergonomics of any wheel prior to purchase. Does it fit you? Are you happy with the method of speed control?

There is, like the small kiln, a small tabletop wheel available. It's a rather clever looking contraption that I have seen potters using while demonstrating at shows and craft fairs; it is also far cheaper than a floor mounted model and ideal for the newcomer.

CLAY

It is advisable to buy clay ready prepared in bags as it is more consistent in quality and texture. A prepared clay is usually called a body.

The main types available are School Buff Smooth, a good all round clay with a smooth surface, it can be fired to earthenware or stoneware. White Stoneware is good for throwing with a high strength in the body. Craft Crank, usually used for hand building, is

A hobbyist's electric wheel is flanked by different clays. The blue banding wheel is used for painting bands of colour.

. . . .

excellent for slab work and coiling. This clay can also be fired to earthenware or stoneware. Most manufacturers also make a Special White Earthenware which is good for most jobs and fires to a clean white finish. Porcelain is more expensive and should only be used by the more experienced. Red terracotta is a good basic body for modelling and for unglazed work.

Other types of clay include decorating slip, a liquid form of clay which has been coloured and which is used for slip trailing. Newclay is a non-firing body and hardens in the air. It can also be baked in a domestic oven or fired in a kiln.

Remember to always keep clay that is not being worked on covered with polythene.

CONSTRUCTION TOOLS

The tools shown here are primarily used in the actual making of your work as opposed to the decoration. **Kidneys**, both metal and rubber, are used for smoothing work; **turning tools** for cleaning up the form on the wheel. A **rolling pin** and **guides** enable you to roll clay to a consistent thickness. The red tool next to the black-handled knife is a **surform** which can be bought from a DIY store; it is useful for cleaning up rough, external edges of plaster moulds. The **modelling tools** are used for similar purposes but the steel tools are particularly useful for modelling leather hard clay and plaster.

The **callipers** will enable you to check the dimensions of a pot while it is being made. **Hole makers** are exactly that - for making consistent-sized holes in the clay. However, a pencil or ballpoint pen can serve equally well.

The **clay cutting needle** is a useful tool for cutting an uneven top rim off a thrown pot. The **cheese wire** will slice off the required portion of clay for your immediate use. It will also remove pots from a wheel head.

Other tools include a **sponge** to smooth down wet clay; a **kitchen scourer** to smooth clay that has dried and **rubber gloves** for when working with plaster. Whatever you do, don't feel compelled to buy the complete kit - build up your tool box gradually and improvise wherever possible.

DISTILLED VINEGAR

SPRAY ON VARNISH

ROLLING PIN

TURNING TOOLS

METAL KIDNEYS

STEEL PALETTE

RUBBER KIDNEY

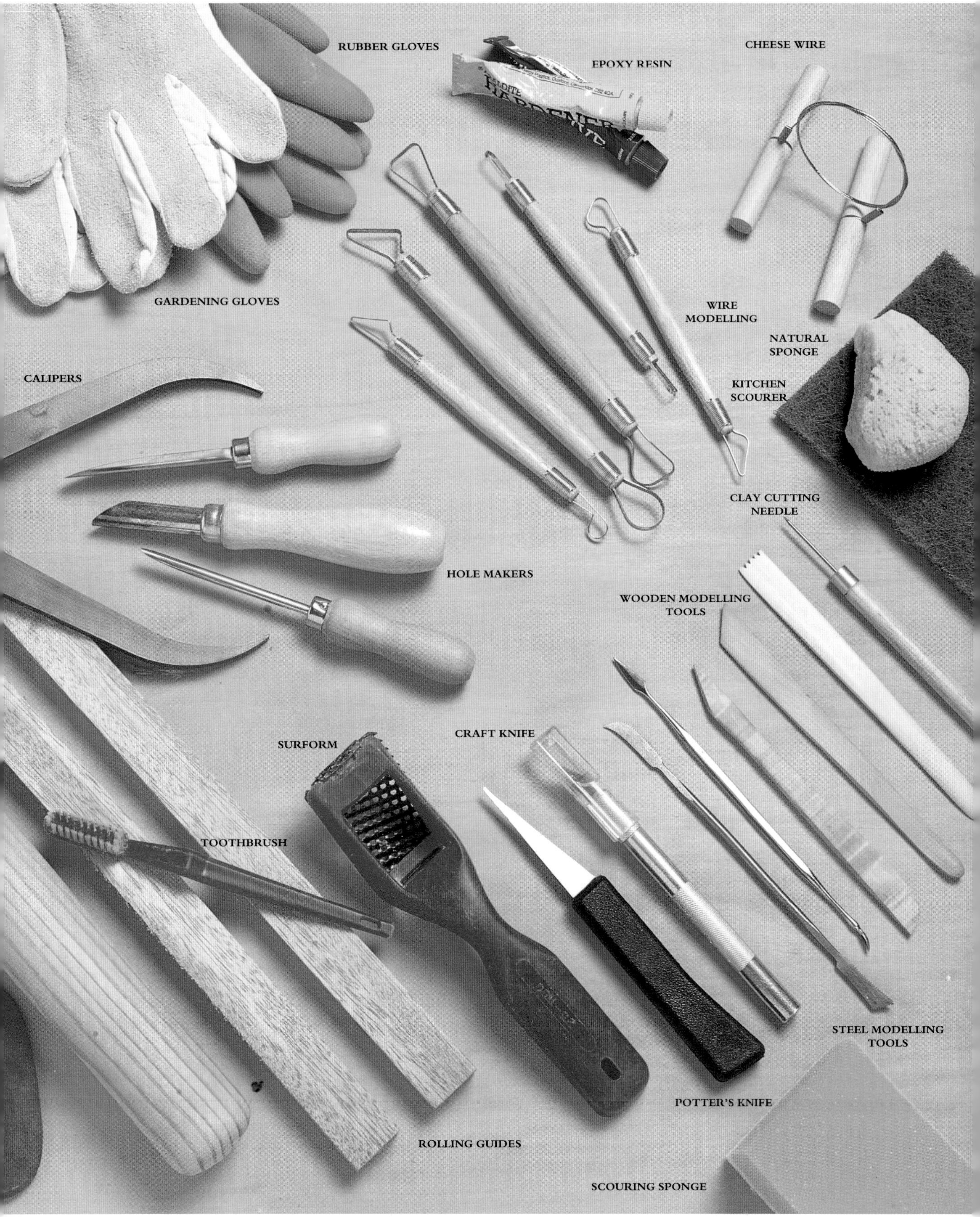

RUBBER GLOVES

EPOXY RESIN

CHEESE WIRE

GARDENING GLOVES

WIRE
MODELLING

NATURAL
SPONGE

CALIPERS

KITCHEN
SCOURER

CLAY CUTTING
NEEDLE

HOLE MAKERS

WOODEN MODELLING
TOOLS

SURFORM

CRAFT KNIFE

TOOTHBRUSH

STEEL MODELLING
TOOLS

POTTER'S KNIFE

ROLLING GUIDES

SCOURING SPONGE

DECORATING TOOLS

This photograph shows the materials and tools used in the decoration of your work.

A good quality **respirator** is a worthwhile investment when working with glazes, as cheap ones become uncomfortable after a short while.

A **slip trailer** is as its names suggests and is used in the wistaria platter on page 88.

Mesh sieves come in a number of grades. The one shown is an 80 mesh sieve; it is used to remove any lumps from powdered glaze. The number printed on the side denotes the amount of holes per square inch, so the higher the number, the finer the mesh. The sieve brush forces the glaze through the mesh.

The group of small pots are brush-on **glazes** and cold ceramic colours. The larger pale blue pot is some crackle glaze and the open bag is lead free transparent glaze in its powder form.

One method of applying glaze is to use a **spray gun**. The larger of the two is of the same type used in car repair workshops. Car parts suppliers are often the cheapest places to buy such a spray gun. You will need to buy an electric air compressor with this type of spray gun as well and these can prove quite expensive. The smaller gun however, operates from a can of compressed air, the initial cost being much lower but, being a hobbyist's tool, it is not as powerful.

The range of **brushes** shown may look daunting at first glance but you will not need all of them for any one project in this book. The stencil brush is - as its name implies - for stencilling designs. Next, is a fan brush which can be used for delicate sweeping strokes; a glaze mop is shown below that and is used for applying brush-on glaze, it has very soft bristles to reduce the chance of brushstrokes remaining on your work. The large round brush is called a sieve brush for forcing mixed glaze or slip through a sieve and the long flat hake brush is employed to apply an even coat of glaze or slip.

The brushes ranged across the bottom of the picture are a sample selection for decorating your work. The exception being the household paintbrush which is used to brush off wax emulsion resist after a bisque firing.

On page 94 you will find a list of suppliers who will be happy to send you a catalogue showing their range of equipment and materials.

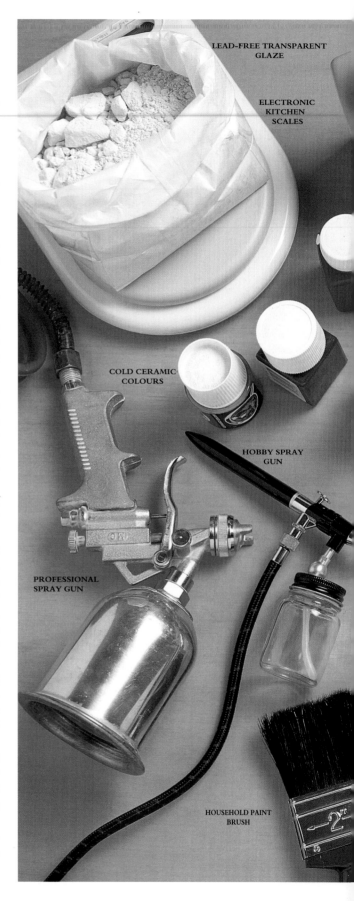

LEAD-FREE TRANSPARENT GLAZE

ELECTRONIC KITCHEN SCALES

COLD CERAMIC COLOURS

HOBBY SPRAY GUN

PROFESSIONAL SPRAY GUN

HOUSEHOLD PAINT BRUSH

CRAKLE GLAZE

80 MESH SIEVE

RESPIRATOR

SLIP TRAILER

BRUSH-ON GLAZES

STENCIL BRUSH

COLD CERAMIC COLOUR

FAN BRUSH

FLAT HAKE BRUSH

GLAZE MOP

SIEVE BRUSH

SCISSORS

RULER

FELT PEN

MASKING TAPE

PENCIL

A SELECTION OF
ARTIST'S BRUSHES

BASIC TECHNIQUES

THE INFORMATION CONTAINED in this section, while by no means the definitive guide, will enable the reader to embark with some confidence on a craft or hobby which may well in time turn into a profession. The following instructions are a starting point.

The techniques utilised in the mastery of pottery is unlike the discipline of learning to drive: there are no rules, no correct way to do it, just a few conventions laid down by old men with beards, bellies and smocks. Ignore them and break any given rules with impunity.

Notwithstanding the above, one rule I do value and follow (most of the time) is the necessity of keeping accurate records of any experiment. If through experimentation or a defying of convention, an innovative reaction, finish or style is achieved, it is exceedingly frustrating if you cannot remember what you did. Remember Louis Pasteur, 'In the field of experimentation, chance favours only the prepared mind'. Good records will enable you to deduce as well as replicate.

WEDGING

As we saw in the last chapter, clay these days is supplied ready mixed and wrapped in manageable sized plastic bags. However, there is some preparatory work; the amount though will be dependent to some extent on the chosen method of construction.

It is essential that the clay is wedged prior to use. Wedging is similar to the practise of the baker, who kneads the dough to introduce air into the mixture to assist rising. Our objective however, is the opposite, we want to expel air from the clay and achieve a smooth consistency and even molecular structure.

There are many favoured methods to achieve this but constraints of space limit me to the two most useful. The Bull's Head method is for smaller amounts and the Spiral method for larger quantities of clay.

The Bull's Head method: use a cheese wire to cut a slice of clay from the block and roll it into a rough ball. Place the ball in front of you on a wooden batt and, using the heels of your palms, push down in one vigorous movement into the centre and roll the clay forward. Keep your fingers outstretched, lift the clay back towards you after each movement.

As you continue, the ball will take on the

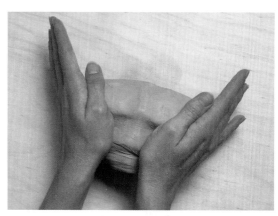

Wedging clay using the Bull's Head method.

. . . .

shape of a fat sausage with a spiral at each end. After a short time, where the heels of the palms are placed, indentations, similar to the cheeks of a bull, will be formed with the spirals representing the horns.

The Spiral method: form a larger ball and with your right hand push down and round in an anti-clockwise direction but off centre. Use your left hand to support the ball and in a short while you should have started to form a point at the base of your clay; the required shape is

Pulling out the wall of a drum to form your pot.

. . . .

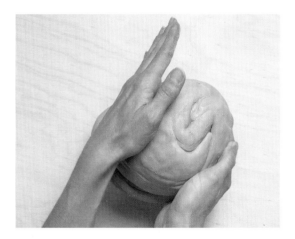

Wedging clay using the spiral method.

. . . .

similar to an old-fashioned wooden top. Use the point as the base while continuing to push and turn the clay until a spiral has clearly formed at the top. Form into a ball: your clay is now ready to be thrown on the wheel or rolled out.

THROWING

Ensure your wheel is clean of all residues and slap the clay on to the wheel head. Centring the clay on a wheel is essential. If this is not done correctly the centrifugal force of the ball of clay spinning at speed will quickly result in the clay being thrown to the side of your wheel.

Wet your hands and use the balls of your thumbs around the clay to gently move the mass into a position where there is no fluctuation and the clay is rotating on its axis. Keep your left arm tucked into your hip and your arm muscles

relaxed. Use water as a lubricant all the time.

Forming the initial shape is always done by pulling up a cone which is then flattened down again into a drum shape. This helps to expel any air and for the novice is a good way of familiarising themselves with the way clay handles on the wheel. Place your finger into the centre of the drum and pull outwards; slow the wheel speed as you pull. Use your left hand to support the wall of the drum.

The next step is to pull up the wall to form a simple cylinder. Place your left hand inside the cavity you formed and your right hand outside the cavity. By applying gentle pressure from your fingertips and at the same time raising your hands, the walls of the drum will rise to form a cylinder. Repeat this until you have achieved the desired height and thickness of the walls.

Use your thumb and two fingers to form a lip for pouring if required. First pull up the area

Pulling up the wall to form a simple cylinder.

. . . .

Forming the spout on the cylinder is quite straightforward.

. . . .

where the spout will be formed. Take care as the walls are fragile and it is easy to split them.

You will need to remove your finished cylinder from the wheel head. Sprinkle a small amount of water over the wheel and then drag a cheese wire under the pot. This is by far the easiest method. Place your work on a wooden batt and leave to firm up. Clean your work with a damp sponge or a turning tool to remove finger marks and irregularities

ROLLING OUT

Prior to using the methods of construction called slabbing or press moulding, you will need to roll out your clay with a rolling pin and two wooden guides. The guides can be bought from a potter's suppliers, but any wood of the required thickness, normally about 4-6 mm (¼ in), will do just as well. Roll out on to a hessian cloth, pushing the clay in front of the rolling pin.

Using a rolling pin and guides to obtain an even thickness.

. . . .

SLABBING

This is a simple and useful method of joining leather hard clay.

Use a serrated kidney, or a knife to score the areas of the joins, then brush a wet toothbrush over the scored lines to 'slurry' the clay. When the walls have been brought together, smooth down the outside join with your fingers. For added strength, a coil of clay may be laid on the inside of the join and then smoothed down.

Three separate slabs, scored and slurried, about to be joined.

. . . .

COILING

Rolling a coil is often thought to be a simple process, whereas in fact, the lightness of touch required to prevent the coil forming a flattened shape takes some practice.

Start with a ball of clay and roll back and forwards on a wooden batt with the palms. As the coil starts to form and decrease in diameter you will need to use your fingertips.

The base plate for a coiled pot is made by simply cutting around a bowl or a dish of some sort which is placed on a rolled out slab. Lay the first coil on to the base, making an angled cut where the join will be. Continue in this fashion until you have four or five coils in place ensuring that each join is never directly over its predecessor. Smooth down both the inside and outside of the coiled pot with a wooden modelling tool or your fingers using vertical strokes. When the pot has become leather hard

Use the bowl as a template for the base of your pot.

. . . .

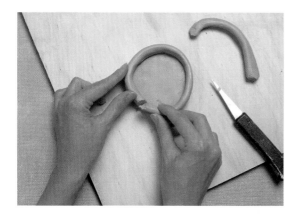

Laying the first coil. Notice the angled cut of the join.

. . . .

The pot begins to form its shape. Note how each coil is joined in a different place.

. . . .

i.e. no longer malleable and plastic but still able to be modelled with ease, you can beat the sides and rim of your pot with a long wooden batt to 'knock' it into shape.

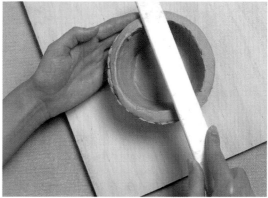

Knock the pot into shape with a wooden batt.

. . . .

PULLING

Coiling can be utilised to form handles for jugs and mugs, but a far superior method is the one shown in the photograph. This is called pulling. It involves having a pear-shaped piece of clay in your left hand and, by using pressure exerted between your thumb and forefinger of your right hand, drawing the clay firmly down. Keep your hand wet and use the fleshy part at the base of your forefinger to form a slightly dished flat

Pulling a handle.

. . . .

surface which, when fitted to a mug, will provide an ergonomic position for the thumb.

PLASTER CASTING

A mould enables many copies of the same object to be produced quickly. Were I to coil every pot I make, they would not be economically viable. Of course I could throw all my bowls and pots but that method severely limits the possible forms. The plaster casting project on pages 30-33 shows the basic principles involved but two things always need to be considered. The first is, are there any 'undercuts' and if so, how to negate them. The second is how to achieve the quickest method of constructing the mould.

Look at the photograph of the glass bottle below, and you will see an area under the bottle blocked in by clay. It is this area that is an undercut. Imagine I were to remove the clay,

Eliminating undercuts prior to casting a small bottle.

. . . .

build my walls (or cottle) as described in the plaster casting project and pour wet plaster over the bottle, the plaster would run into the area occupied by the clay in the photograph. When set, the plaster would have totally encased the bottle except the small strip that would have been resting on the table. It would be impossible to remove the bottle from the plaster sarcophagus. To avoid this you must place clay in such a manner that all undercuts are eliminated. This means of course that you can only cast half a bottle, but two halves can be joined together to make a whole clay bottle.

For a piece of a predetermined shape, such as

the pump housing for the fountain on page 84, it is much quicker to just take a solid lump of clay, mould and beat it into the shape required and pour plaster over it. Not only is it quick and easy, but you can then make as many pieces as you choose from the same mould. Having said that, if you wish to cast objects with a fine detailing, the detail in the plaster will begin to wear down after about 30 pressings and the mould should be re-cast.

MODELLING

Of course not everything you may wish to cast can be found on the shelves of shops or on the beach. A case in point is the seahorses used in the pedestal pot on page 72. A real seahorse would be a nightmare of undercuts and they are not particularly attractive creatures when dead. So I modelled one, investing it with my own interpretation of what a seahorse should look like. Use your fingers and any other tools to hand. On the one in the photograph, the eye was formed with the plastic cap of a ballpoint pen, the pupil by the nib. A steel modelling tool forms the skin texture and fins. As soon as you are satisfied with the form, cast it.

The more detail you introduce in your modelling, the better the finished result will be.

. . . .

GLAZING

Glaze comes in powder form, ready mixed with water or in brush-on form. The brush-on type is usually far more expensive than the others as one is paying for the convenience. The manufacturer mixes an additive into brush-on glazes which prevents them appearing streaky .

If you buy glaze in a powder form you will have to add water until it achieves the consistency of single cream. The resulting mixture must then be passed through a 120 mesh sieve. Should you wish to add colour to a clear glaze powder or alter the colour of a manufacturer's powder glaze, you should add the colourant before the water.

If you decide to spray your glaze mixture, be careful not to apply it too thickly as this will make it crawl, craze or run down the side of your pot when fired.

For you own safety when mixing or spraying glaze, you should always wear a respirator. Spraying should always take place in a spray booth fitted with an extractor.

For dipping a pot, the glaze will need to be much thinner in consistency than that mixed for spraying. The photograph below shows the inside of a toothbrush holder filled with glaze. The glaze has dripped down the outside but this is not a problem as you can wipe it off with a damp sponge. Pour the glaze back into the bowl and leave the mug to dry. Use your first and forefingers in the method shown in the photograph above; submerge the mug carefully into the glaze mixture, taking care not to let glaze run over the rim. Touch up any missed areas with a brush.

Glazing the outside of a pot using the dipping method.

. . . .

Underglaze, like normal glaze, comes both in liquid and powder forms; again it is mixed with water but you apply it at the bone dry stage, covering it with a transparent glaze after your pot has been bisque fired.

Lustre, as used by Susie Lear in her theatre clock project on page 54 is always applied in a third firing at a much lower temperature.

A word of caution, if you choose to use any lead-based glazes (I never do, nor do any of the projects in this book), do not mix copper oxides or copper carbonites with the lead on work that may be used for food or drink.

FIRING

Most work will entail two firings. The first, called a bisque or biscuit firing is done when the pot has become bone dry. The temperatures and the rate of 'ramp' will vary according to the type of clay used. The term ramp is used to define the rate of increase in the temperature in the kiln. Start off slowly to allow any small amounts of moisture remaining in the pot to be expelled as steam without running the risk of the pot exploding.

The secondary firing is called the glaze or glost firing, the object being to melt the glaze and fuse it to the body of the pot. This will result in a waterproof surface.

A third firing, if used, is for decorative applications such as transfers (Decals) on glaze painting lustres.

Glazing the inside of a pot using the dipping method is simple and straightforward.

. . . .

GALLERY

On the following pages, I illustrate some of the contemporary work of ceramicists whose work I admire and in some cases collect. Some of the work is made on a commercial basis and others are one-off products and only available from specialist galleries. The unifying factor is that all the people featured are professional, and their work is of a high standard. They reached those standards by perseverance and diligence. The object of the Gallery is to inspire and encourage you to persevere yourself and to look at clay as an inexhaustible canvas for experimentation and your own artistic development.

~

Part of the Neptune Collection
LIZA GARDNER
It is hard for me to comment objectively about my own work other than to say I am particularly proud of the colour responses obtained with this range. I use cobalt and copper with repeated firings, laying glaze on glaze, until I achieve the depth of colour I require.

Thrown Shallow Bowl

SARAH PERRY

Sarah is a potter because she enjoys the basic feel of clay, its versatility and the actual making process. She revels in the fact that a piece can be stopped at any point while it is being worked and made permanent by firing. She says, 'It's rather like making the stones under one's feet'. This beautiful bowl measures 30 cm (12 in) in diameter.

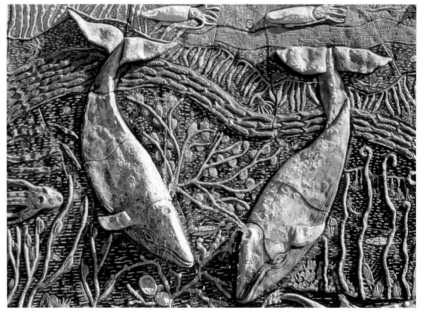

Whale Fountain and Waterfall (detail)

MARIA ALQUILAR

This work was commissioned by the water company in Sacramento, California. Most of the artist's work is site specific and she uses images that relate to the placing of her work. Maria uses underglaze colours, building up layers of colour until the piece is coated with a transparent glaze.

Casket

LAURANCE SIMON

Much of Laurance's work is inspired by her travels in India and East Africa. The jumble of images she collects all eventually find their way into her work in some way, as in the modelling for the handle of this supremely individual piece.

Isis Vase

RIMMINGTON★VIAN

Rimmington★Vian is a partnership between Kevin Rimmington and Phillip Vian. This piece has a pale blue and lilac slip which has a sgraffito decoration revealing the white body underneath. The precision in their work is stunning; the two bands of platinum lustre, which has been crackled, gives the vase an individual touch.

Ahten Plate

RIMMINGTON★VIAN

As with the Isis Vase on page 25, the decoration is the same with much finer detail in the centre of the plate. Each cut into the slip is made by eye, and the segments are all drawn freehand.

Anger (part of The Seven Deadly Sins)

JANICE TCHALENCKO/ SPITTING IMAGE WORKSHOP

A joint venture between these artists resulted in a stunning collection of modern ceramics. The pieces are on display at the Victoria and Albert Museum in London.

Vision 1

BARBARA SEBASTIAN

This wall piece (below) is constructed from shards of fired clay pressed into fresh clay. The slab is then low-fired and fixed to a wooden backplate. The colours are achieved with acrylic paints applied on to abstract images which, the artist believes, reflect archaeological segments found in the contemporary world.

Morwenna 1

GILLIAN HODGE

The image of Morwenna - a seductive mermaid - has been Gillian's inspiration for many years and she has sculpted her often.

Teapot, Cream Jug and Spoon

JESSICA BALL

These pieces are made by using slabs of thinly rolled clay which is then surface decorated. Lustre adds a crisp finish to the floral design.

Vase

SUSIE LEAR

Similar to the theatre clock on page 54, Susie has used the same technique of applying lustre as small dots to this entertaining piece. The whimsical shape of the vase is constructed from slabs of clay pressed into a mould.

Piscean Basin

LIZA GARDNER

This hand basin is a development from the bowl shown on the front cover. The size was increased and a hole was added for the plug along with an overflow system. A satisfying, if technically challenging, item.

Plate

GENEVIEVE NIELSON
Exploding parrot tulips
is how this plate is
described by Genevieve.
It was thrown on a
wheel with the
decoration method
being the same as that
on her ewer on page 42.
The vivid colours and
freedom in the fluid
brushstrokes can only be
greatly admired.

Knotted Tree

JEFF IRWIN
A sculptural work with
an intended narrative, it
is open to a number of
ecological
interpretations. The
work is hand built in
white earthenware with
vitreous white slip
applied after a bisque
firing. A further
application of black slip
is applied over wax
resist giving a clean line.
A final firing creates a
satin finish.

FOUND OBJECTS

LIZA GARDNER

To decorate the famous blue and white Jasper ware pots, Joshia Wedgwood employed the sculptor John Flaxman to sculpt a small relief which was then cast in bronze. A plaster cast was made and a small amount of clay pressed into the mould and carefully lifted out. These clay decorations were called sprigs and the technique of applying them became known as sprigging. This method is still in use in the Wedgwood factory today.

Not everybody is a skilled modeller or sculptor, but by using this technique of casting a found object, you will be able to decorate your work with an array of three-dimensional motifs limited only by your imagination. The items cast are everyday things, such as shells or small architectural motifs.

Plaster casting is a simple technique to master and once learnt will allow you to embark upon some of the more challenging projects in this book. The principle is just the same to cast a mould for a bowl, dish or a plate. The result is a cast which will enable you to make as many sprigs or items as you require.

~

MATERIALS AND EQUIPMENT

• *jug* • *bucket* • *potter's plaster* • *white earthenware clay* • *potter's needle* • *modelling tool* • *petroleum jelly* • *wooden boards* • *cardboard* • *parcel or masking tape* • *metal rasp* • *various found objects* • *shells* • *brass architectural details* • *rubber gloves*

. . . . . .

1 Select the objects you wish to cast and ensure they are clean and dust free. Take a wooden board and roll out a slab of clay thick enough to receive the impressions of the objects you wish to cast. Lay your objects on the slab. Any item having an undercut will need to be embedded into the clay slab.

Ensure that you embed the item deep enough to lose any such undercut. To embed the item just draw around it with a potters' needle or similar tool and gouge out the slab with a modelling tool, place the item into the cavity and smooth the surface of the slab down with your fingers.

2 Apply a thin layer of petroleum jelly to the surface of the objects and the clay slab. This stops the objects sticking to the plaster. Make sure you apply a thin, even coat as any blobs will obscure the detail of your cast.

3 Construct a wall of cardboard or of wooden slats around the clay slab. This wall should be high enough to cover the objects with an additional 25 mm (1 in) clearance. You should use some tape to bind the walls together and then secure the base of the walls using coils of clay.

4 Fill a jug or bowl with water and slowly add plaster by sprinkling it over the surface of the water until it has absorbed most of the water and can be seen as a peak coming through the surface. Leave to settle for 5 minutes and then mix thoroughly. Pour the mixture over the objects and dab the final surface with your hands to remove any air bubbles. Lay aside to set. As the plaster begins to set it will become quite warm; this is purely a chemical reaction and is quite normal.

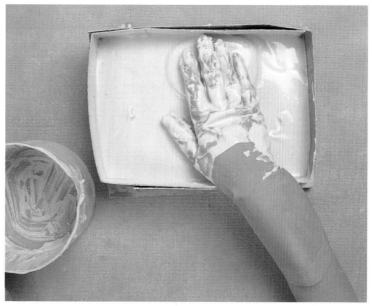

5 When fully set, an hour or more depending on the thickness of your mould, remove the walls you constructed, turn over the mould and peel away the clay slab. Some objects will be retained by the plaster and some by the clay. Clean up any rough edges of the plaster with a surform or a similar rasp. The clay should now be disposed of or put aside and only used for further plaster work as it will have become contaminated.

6 Gently remove the shells and objects from the plaster, taking care not to damage the detailing or the edges of the cast.

FOUR FISH SALAD BOWL

LIZA GARDNER

SEVERAL YEARS AGO, I was asked to design a bowl with a fish theme for a cook book to be published by a well known chain of food retailers. The main criteria was that I devise some decoration which could remain visible when the bowl was full. I decided to make fish chase each others tails, something I had seen in rivers. The idea of extending the rim of the bowl to make the silhouette of the fish's dorsal fin just seemed to be one of those happy stokes of luck that happen every so often. This bowl has been one of my best sellers ever since!

I have drawn the design directly into the clay, a method known as incising. This should not be confused with sgraffito, a similar method except that sgraffito reveals another colour under the cut line. To accentuate the bodies of the fishes I have used a contrasting glaze to the main part of the bowl.

～

MATERIALS AND EQUIPMENT

- *rolling pin* • *rolling guides*
- *plaster mould of a medium sized bowl with a rim*
- *white earthenware clay*
- *kiln* • *old credit card*
- *tracing paper* • *stiff card template* • *bowl* • *sponge*
- *craft knife* • *rubber kidney*
- *pencil* • *banding wheel*
- *rutile underglaze*
- *respirator* • *hobby spray gun and compressed air*
- *lead-free transparent glaze in blue and green*

. . . . . .

1 Roll out a slab of clay about 3 mm (⅛ in) thick (see page 18). Using a damp sponge, press the slab into the plaster mould, smooth with a rubber kidney and trim the rim to the edge of your mould. Using the old credit or phone card smooth the rim until it is flat and level.

2 Trace off the template on page 92 and transfer it to stiff card. Place the template in the centre of the bowl and carefully cut around the edge with a sharp craft knife. Smooth down the edges of the cuts with a damp sponge and leave till leather hard.

3 Draw in the shape of the fish and the scales with a blunt pencil; keep an even pressure and draw freely. Carefully, brush away any loose or raised clay with a damp sponge

4 Using a small paint brush colour the fins, tail and eyes with rutile underglaze. Allow to dry and then bisque fire to 1120° C (2048° F).

5 Now you can apply the glaze. If you have never used a spray gun before, practise first! Use even strokes without pausing, especially at the end of a stroke. Glaze the body of the fish using the blue transparent glaze.

Change colour to the green glaze and glaze the back of the bowl. Turn the bowl over the right way up and spray the green glaze around the bodies of the fish and the middle of the bowl. Glaze does not normally appear as it is

shown here, but I have added some food colouring to make it clearer. The pink represents the blue and the pale blue is the green glaze. Wipe the foot ring clean with a damp sponge and fire to 1060–1080° C (1940° F).

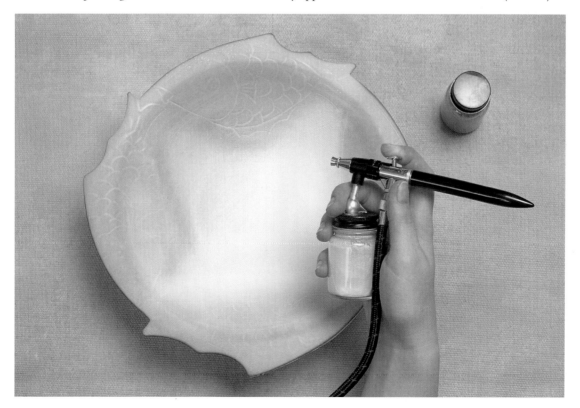

NIGHT LIGHT

SAM FARAWAY

NIGHT LIGHTS, OIL BURNERS and the like are a regular source of income for the prosaic studio potter, however they do not have to be the usual mundane shape and any innovative or whimsical design features can be integrated into the basic functional form.

Sam's inspiration for this shape stems from his interest in Islamic design and alchemy, two disparate influences that he has successfully fused into one. The basic shape is simple and stable to throw on a wheel, having little chance of collapsing. It is a shape which is also evocative of the spires and minarets of the East.

Crackle glaze has been used on the exterior of the piece to resemble tile mosaic.

When alight, the night light will cast intricate shadows on the walls and the flickering light within has the mystique of an alchemist's still.

~

MATERIALS AND EQUIPMENT

* *potter's wheel* * *wooden batt* * *white earthenware clay*
* *scales* * *kiln* * *bowl*
* *sponge* * *craft knife*
* *metal kidney* * *turning tool*
* *cheese wire* * *card*
* *scissors* * *banding wheel*
* *fine modelling tool*
* *glaze mop* * *flat brush*
* *brush-on lrackle glaze*
* *brush-on deep blue glaze*
* *Indian ink*
* *night light candle*

. . . . . .

1 Weigh out a 500 g (1 lb) ball of clay and throw a pot on your potter's wheel with a wooden batt on the wheel head. Your pot should have a 14 cm (5 ½ in) diameter base. Pull up to a conical shape about 10 cm 4 in) high. Clean up any finger marks with a metal kidney.

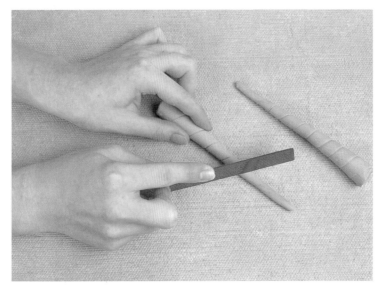

2 Roll out a tapered coil which will form a finial for your night light. Using a ruler held at 45 degrees to the coil, roll the coil while pressing down on the ruler to create a spiral indentation into the clay. Bend the coil into a pleasing shape. Add a small coil to the base of the bent one.

3 Using a sharp craft knife, cut some shapes from some mediumweight paper. These will form the cut-out portions of your night light and will determine the shape of the shadows cast by the candle. Do not make the shapes too intricate or place them too close together as this will weaken the structure. When you have cut out the shapes, place them on the pot and gently press into the clay to leave a slight depression in the surface. Remove the paper shapes with the craft knife. Leave to dry until leather hard. Cut a hole at the back, large enough to allow a night light candle to pass freely into the interior.

4 The depressions left in the clay surface are the guidelines for you to know where to cut out the clay with a craft knife.

5 Place the finial on the top of the pot using a small amount of water to slurry the join. With a fine modelling tool you can now add surface detailing. Sam has scored some simple squiggles to the apexes of his cut-outs. Leave till bone dry and then bisque fire to 1,100° C. (2012° F)

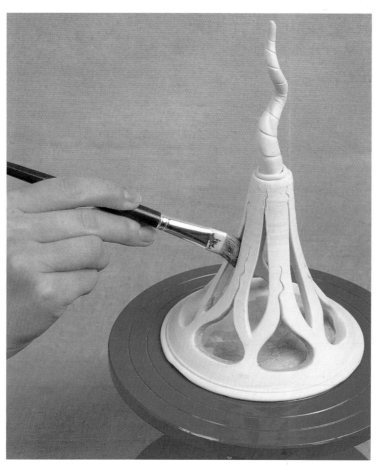

6 Glaze the inside with the dark blue brush-on glaze using a flat brush, also glaze the edges of the cut outs. Lightly touch the uppermost part of the squiggles with a blob of glaze, allowing the blue to run down the lines. Leave to dry for 10 minutes. Brush on the crackle glaze liberally with a soft glaze mop. Fire to 1060° C (1940° F). When completely cool, remove from the kiln and rub some Indian ink into the surface with a soft cloth. This will accentuate the crazing of the glaze.

TALL EWER ON STAND

GENEVIEVE NIELSON

THE SHAPE OF THIS EWER IS A CLEVER adaptation of a classical vessel known as an amphora. Usually this would be a large container for wine with a handle on either side and a base forming a point which would have been placed in a depression in the ground or in an ornamental ring. Here, one of the handles has been removed, a spout has been formed and the vessel has been mounted on a thrown base.

The distinctive method of decoration is known as wax resist, a simple way of overlaying colours to give crisp outlines on contrasting tones with little danger of the colours running or smearing. The oranges and foliage in this particular piece were inspired by a visit to the Alhambra Palace in Granada, Spain. You can, of course, adapt the technique of decoration used in this project for a smaller vase or a bowl.

~

MATERIALS AND EQUIPMENT

- white earthenware clay
- potter's wheel • kiln
- 2 wooden batts • callipers
- banding wheel • large
bucket • large plastic bag
- toothbrush • knife • metal
kidney • smooth-ended
boxwood modelling tool
- half round turning tool
- sponge • cheese wire
- soft-bristled decorating brush
- 25 mm (1 in) flat-ended
brush • 2 x 18 mm (¾ in)
flat-ended brushes • soft
pencil • clear lead free
earthenware glaze (with high
craze resistance) • underglaze
stain in bright orange, mid
green, pale green, cobalt blue
- wax emulsion resist

. . . . . .

1 Throw the shape to create a jug. Pull the spout forward using your thumb and forefinger and put to one side. Throw the base on a wooden batt. When both items have become leather hard, turn the base to fit the jug. This is best achieved on the wheel head. Centre the base and fix in place with three blobs of clay. Rotate your wheel slowly and remove any excess clay with the turning tool until you have a good fit between the jug and the base. Gauge the dimensions with callipers. Remove the base and tidy the foot ring. Replace the base on the wheel head, centring and fixing as before.

2 Using a toothbrush, slurry the bottom of your jug and the top of the base; join them together. Clean up the join with a turning tool as before and finish off with a damp sponge to remove any marks left by the tool. Also clean the inside of the base by turning the whole jug upside down. Turn the jug the right way up, correct any distortion that may have occurred, and leave to firm up on a dry wooden batt while loosely wrapped in a large plastic bag.

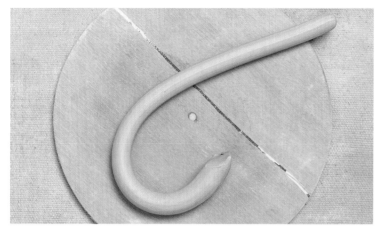

3 Roll out a coil for the handle about 18 mm (¾ in) in diameter, remembering to leave additional length on the coil to allow for the angled cuts you must make. You can, if you wish, pull the handle; this is a more difficult technique than coiling but will give a more professional look to your jug. Lay the coil out in the shape required. Leave until leather hard.

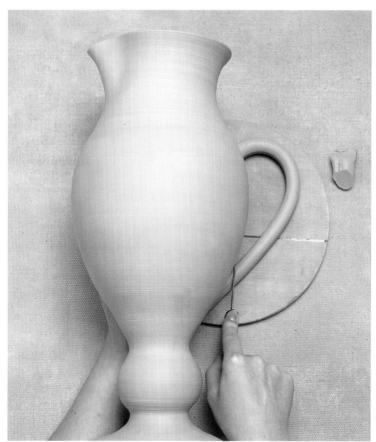

4 Hold the jug horizontally in front of you, directly over the laid-out handle. Sight the lines of intersection on the handle, where the top and bottom abut the edge of the jug. Cut the handle carefully at these two points, making sure that you follow the shape of the jug.

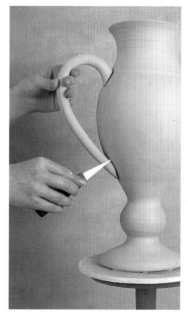

5 Place your jug, still on the wooden batt, on to a banding wheel. Line up the handle opposite the spout and check for vertical alignment. Using your knife, mark the position of the joining points top and bottom on each side of the handle.

6 Slurry between the knife marks you have made and the handle ends with a toothbrush. Join the handle to the jug with firm pressure while supporting the inside wall of the jug to avoid any distortion. Clean up the joins with a smooth-ended boxwood tool and then sponge. Leave loosely wrapped for a day or so then unwrap and allow to become bone dry.

Decoration

7 Place the jug on a banding wheel, taking great care as it is extremely fragile at this stage. Use the soft pencil to draw the design directly on to the jug. Don't worry about the lines you make, as these will burn off when you fire the jug. To create the oranges, draw bold circles in a pleasing arrangement.

8 Using a bright orange underglaze stain generously loaded on to a 18 mm (¾ in) flat ended soft brush, fill in the outlines of the oranges.

9 Now paint over all the oranges with a separate 18 mm (¾ in) brush loaded with liquid wax resist.

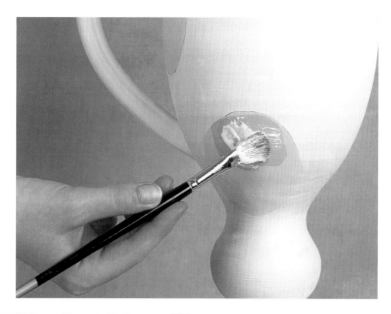

10 Take a large flat-ended brush about 25 mm (1 in) across and, using the palest green, paint in the first layer of the foliage. Wipe your brush on the edge of the glaze container to ensure that you do not put too much colour on to the pot as the underglaze is very thin and watery. Should you experience runs in the colour, these can be wiped away with a damp cloth. Repeat the wax resist process as for the oranges.

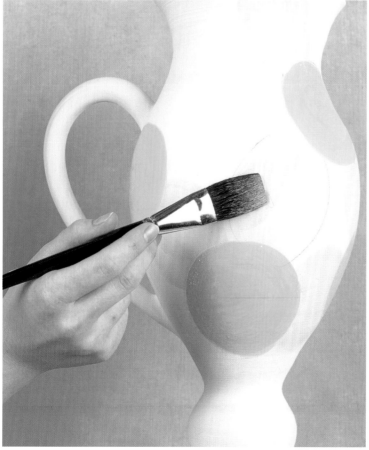

11 Clean the brush used for the light green and paint on the darker green that is the colour designated for the second layer of foliage. Apply the wax resist as before.

12 Using a metal kidney, scratch off the wax resist to create small areas, such as the highlights on the oranges, which will take your background colour. Then liberally apply the background colour, in this case, cobalt blue. Use a large brush to cover the entire jug including the inside and the handle. Don't worry about painting over the oranges or leaves as the wax resist will stop the background colour obscuring them. Remember,that the jug remains extremely fragile, so take great care must be taken.

13 Bisque fire to 1,000° C (1832° F) in a well ventilated room, preferably with an extractor. The wax burns off at about 190° C, (374° F), a process that lasts for about an hour. When the kiln has fully cooled, withdraw your jug and, using a soft decorator's brush and making sure you are wearing a respirator, brush off the wax residue which looks like a fine white ash.

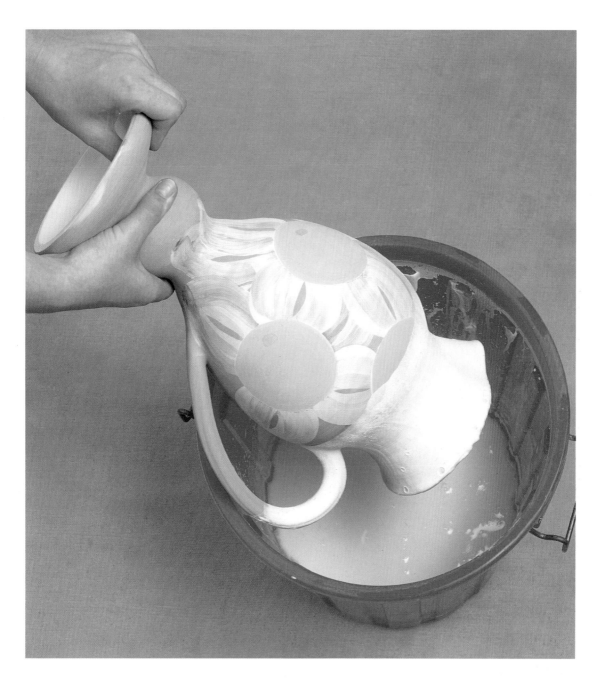

14 Pour some earthenware clear glaze, preferably with a high craze resistance, into the inside of the jug and pour the glaze out again whilst rotating the jug to ensure that the inside of the jug is completely covered with glaze. Invert the jug and dip the top half into a large bucket of glaze. With your hand inside the jug, dip the bottom half into the glaze bucket. Touch up any missed or smudged areas of glaze with a small brush. Clean off the glaze on the foot ring with a damp sponge and fire to 1120° C (2048° F).

PAINTED PLATE

LIZA GARDNER

THIS PROJECT REQUIRES just the most basic of materials and can easily be undertaken by anyone with a steady hand. The paints are called cold ceramic colours. They can be intermixed and thinned, and a basic set of about six colours should be enough to get anyone started.

The stained glass work of Louis Comfort Tiffany provided the initial inspiration for this piece, with a nod towards Charles Rennie Mackintosh, the Scottish designer and architect.

Most discount stores sell plain white china items at very low prices. This type of china is known as whiteware and the pieces are usually slight seconds. You can find a range of plates, cups and dishes, all of which (like the little pot below) can be painted successfully. However, never use the items for food or drink or subject them to your dishwasher!

1 Either copy the design
shown here or draw one of
your own using books,
magazines, giftwrap, postcards
or natural things such as leaves
or flowers as your inspiration.
Trace this design on to some
tracing paper. Ensure the plate
is clean and grease free by
wiping it with white spirit. Cut
a sheet of carbon paper into a
circle the same size as the plate,
fix it on to the plate with some
masking tape and lay the traced
design on top. Trace around
the lines with a sharp pencil;
this will leave an image of the
design on the plate. Remove
the tracing paper and carbon
and draw over the lines with a
permanent marker. This will
give you a good smudge-free
outline to follow.

2 Apply the first ceramic colour
to the rose using a well-
loaded brush and making sure
that the white of the plate does
not show through. Try not to
paint over the black marker lines.
Allow the colour to dry for one
hour; do not touch the surface of
the paint during this time as any
fingerprints will remain. Clean
the brush straight away with
white spirit.

4 Colour in the leaves using brush strokes along the length of the leaves. As before, leave for an hour to dry and clean your brush well in white spirit.

3 Colour in the remaining sections of the roses. Here, three different reds have been used for the blooms, but as the paints are mixable you can devise as many colours as you wish. As before, leave time between each colour and clean your brush in white spirit.

5 Paint in the outlines with black cold ceramic colour. This will enhance the stained glass effect. When finished, leave to dry for at least 24 hours. The paints used in this project are purely for decorative purposes and must not be used in conjunction with food. They can be wiped clean with a damp cloth but should not be put in a dishwasher.

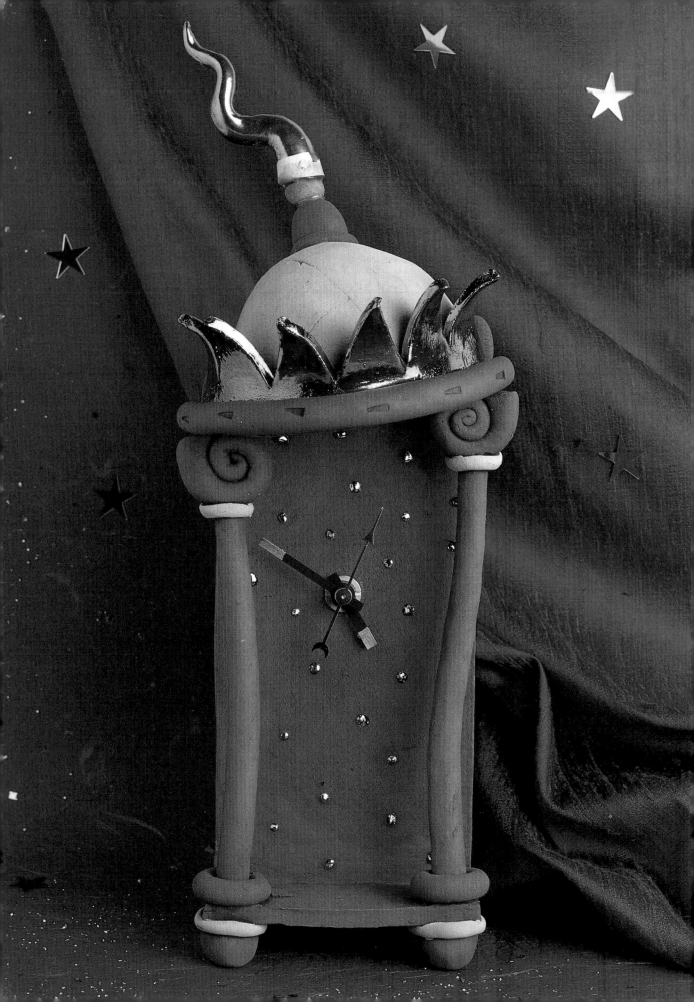

THEATRE CLOCK

SUSIE LEAR

ON APRIL 26, 1994, the Liberty store in London opened an exhibition in the British Craft Room to commemorate the birthday of William Shakespeare. The buyer, Mr Lance Bowmer, selected 28 artists to represent Shakespeare's plays, sonnets and life. Susie Lear was invited to participate in this exhibition and this clock was the result of her research into medieval buildings and English theatre history.

At this time, the reconstruction of William Shakespeare's Globe Theatre was nearing completion and Susie chose to draw on this event to make a clock based on a theatre.

The front pediment of the clock was inspired by an old photograph of a well known actor's crown in a production of Richard III, the clock face was taken from a form of theatrical backdrop known as a 'star cloth', with the main body of the clock being a stylized representation of a theatre.

Although Susie was working to a brief, you could, of course, take a local building and interpret it and its historical connections in a similar manner.

~

MATERIALS AND EQUIPMENT

- *white earthenware clay*
- *red terracotta clay*
- *banding wheel* • *wooden board* • *long thin batt*
- *rolling pin* • *rolling guides*
- *bowl* • *sponge*
- *toothbrush* • *knife*
- *serrated metal kidney*
- *steel modelling tool with arrow and small screwdriver-shaped heads* • *no 2 and no 6 paintbrushes* • *10 mm (½ in) wooden dowel*
- *3 mm (⅛ in) drill bit*
- *25 mm (1 in) panel pin*
- *kiln* • *clear lead-free earthenware glaze in glossy and satin matt finishes*
- *underglaze stain in royal blue and pale green*
- *lustre in copper and gold*
- *fast-drying epoxy resin glue*
- *battery operated clock movement*

. . . . . .

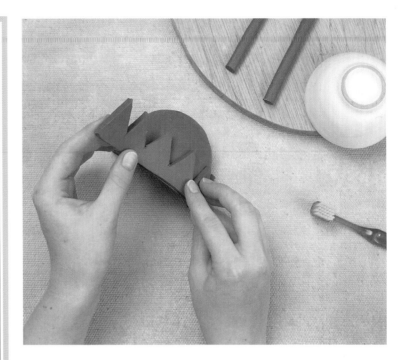

1 First roll out a large slab of terracotta about 4 mm (¼ in) thick and cut out all the shapes required (see patterns on page 93) except the base piece, which should be cut from a slightly thicker piece of clay. Roll out two coils for the pillars about 30 cm x 9 mm (12 x ⅜ in) and lay aside. You will also need to make the dome which will be a quarter of a sphere. Form the dome by using a plaster press mould or a small bowl like the one in the photograph. Then fit the crown shape on to the dome using a toothbrush with some water to score and slurry.

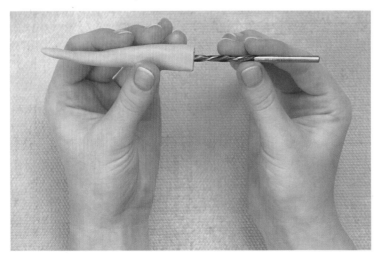

2 Making sure your worktop and hands are clean, and that there is no trace of the red terracotta, take the white earthenware and roll a small tapered coil which will form the finial. Using the drill bit, make a hole in the base about 12 mm (½ in) deep and lay aside.

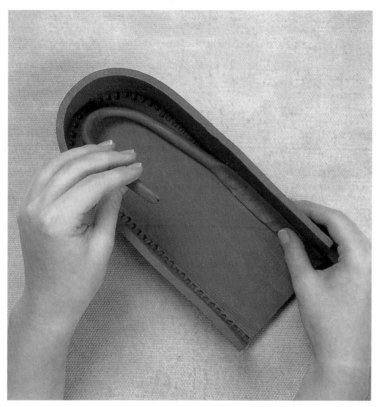

3 Score and slurry one edge of the side wall and the outer portion of the clock face. Fit the side wall to the clock face using a steel modelling tool to push the pieces together. Place a small coil over the indentations made with the modelling tool and smooth down with your finger.

4 Take the base slab, which should be slightly thicker for strength, and place the wall and face sections on to the base. Slurry, use the modelling tool and place a coil over the join as before. Punch out a hole with the dowel rod in the centre of the clock face. Pat down the entire form with a long wooden batt to straighten and square it.

5 Fit the back by placing it under the clock, mark the outline with a knife and cut to fit. (The wall of this clock is designed to be slightly irregular in shape; it is part of its charm.) Score, slurry and join as before, using two coils to cover the joins on the inside of the form.

6 Roll out two coils 6 x 60 mm (¼ x 2 ½ in), two coils 3 x 60 mm (⅛ x 2 ½ in), one coil 3 mm x 30 cm (⅛ x 12 in), five balls about 15 mm (⅝ in) in diameter and two cubes 12 mm (½ in) on all faces. Next, roll two tapered coils which will form the capitals of the columns and one long coil which will need to be tapered at each end. The tapers on these three coils are rolled back on to the coil to form shapes like snail shells.

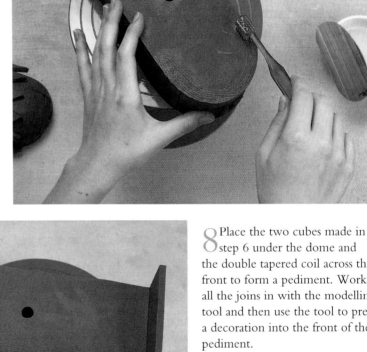

7 By this time the pillars, crown and the dome that you made in step 1 should be leather hard. Score and slurry the dome to take the crown and clean up with a sponge. Lay the clock on its back. Using the serrated kidney, score the face of the clock to receive the dome, slurry with a toothbrush and fit the dome securely in place.

8 Place the two cubes made in step 6 under the dome and the double tapered coil across the front to form a pediment. Work all the joins in with the modelling tool and then use the tool to press a decoration into the front of the pediment.

9 Place one of the five balls made in step 6 on the top of the dome, working it in with the tool and use a small coil to cover the join. Press a hole into the ball at the top with the drill bit. The hole should be about 12 mm (½ in) deep.

10 Score and slurry the top of the pillars and join the two tapered coils concealing the join with a small coil.

11 Join these two pillars to the cubes under the dome and cut the pillars to the correct length. Join the pillars to the base and fit the remaining four balls to the base. Use the modelling tool to work in the joins and cover the marks you have made with small coils as before.

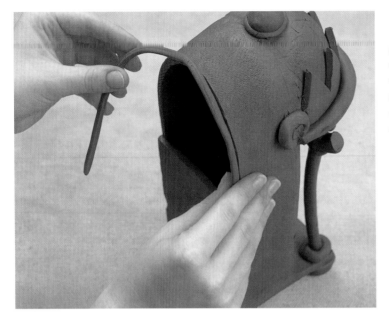

12 Lift the clock up to a vertical position, taking great care as it is extremely fragile at this stage. Place a small ball of clay under the centre of the base as added support and stand the clock upright. Fit the long coil around the back.

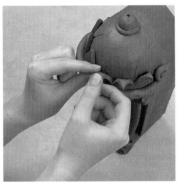

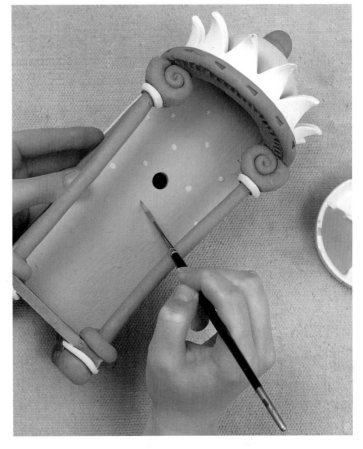

13 Turn out the points of the crown. Remove the small support ball from underneath. Tidy up the clock with a damp sponge and leave till bone dry. Bisque fire to 1020° C (1868° F).

14 Apply the underglaze colours using a small brush. Apply clear brush-on glaze to the front of the crown and clear matt glaze to the finial. Dot the area of the clock face with the same glaze. Glaze fire to 1060° C (1940° F).

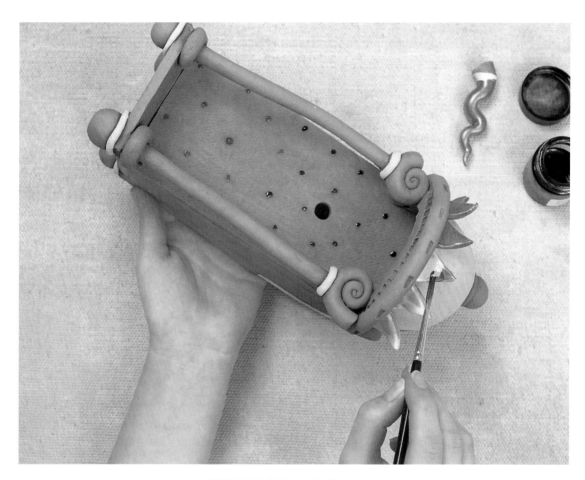

15 When completely cool, paint lustre on to the areas clear glazed in the last step: gold on the crown front and the dots on the face, and copper on the finial. Fire according to the manufacturer's instructions (about 640–700° C/1184–1292° F).

16 Using some epoxy resin, glue the finial to the ball on top of the clock, placing the panel pin in the drilled holes for additional support. Next, fit the clock movement into the hole in the face of the clock, using the retaining nut to hold it firmly in place, and finally fit the hands.

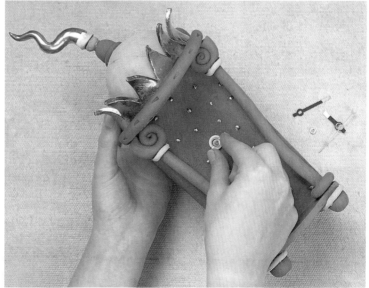

FISH MIRROR

LIZA GARDNER

ONE OF THE GREAT attractions of ceramics is its versatility. Many potters seem to restrict their work unnecessarily to vases, bowls, mugs and such like, but this stylish mirror is one way of making something different out of this extraordinary material. It combines an elegant form with a precise function.

As is usual for my work, I have used motifs from the ocean to decorate my mirror; this does not preclude you from choosing anything you may wish to draw upon, of course. One important point to remember, however, is that to prevent cracking or warping of your mirror frame, limit the size to about 30 cm (12 in) in any one direction.

~

MATERIALS AND EQUIPMENT

- *white earthenware clay*
- *rolling pin and guides*
- *wooden batt* ● *bowl*
- *sponge* ● *craft knife*
- *kitchen scourer*
- *rectangular metal kidney*
- *thin card* ● *pencil* ● *plaster moulds as on page 30* ● *kiln*
- *brush-on lead free transparent glazes in blue and green* ● *glaze mop* ● *mirror, cut to size* ● *old credit card*
- *gloves* ● *epoxy resin adhesive* ● *D ring*
- *masking tape*

· · · · · ·

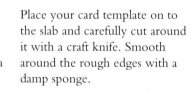

1 Using some thin card, draw a design similar to the one shown in the photograph. It is not necessary that you copy this design, as your own lines will be just as effective. Use a craft knife to cut out the main central hole and the smaller holes near the edge. Roll out a slab of clay between your guides and lay on a large wooden batt. Smooth the surface with a metal kidney. Place your card template on to the slab and carefully cut around it with a craft knife. Smooth around the rough edges with a damp sponge.

2 Select the moulds you wish to use for the sprigging (see page 30) and fill with clay. Place the sprigs in position on the slab, making sure you leave space at the top for the fish (or other motifs) that will be formed later. One by one remove the sprigs, slurry the clay with a wet toothbrush and reposition, gently pushing each one into place.

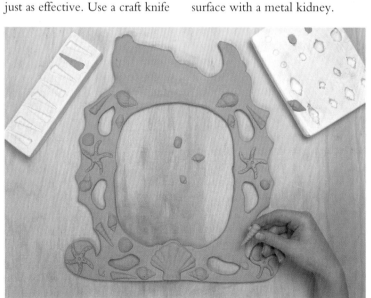

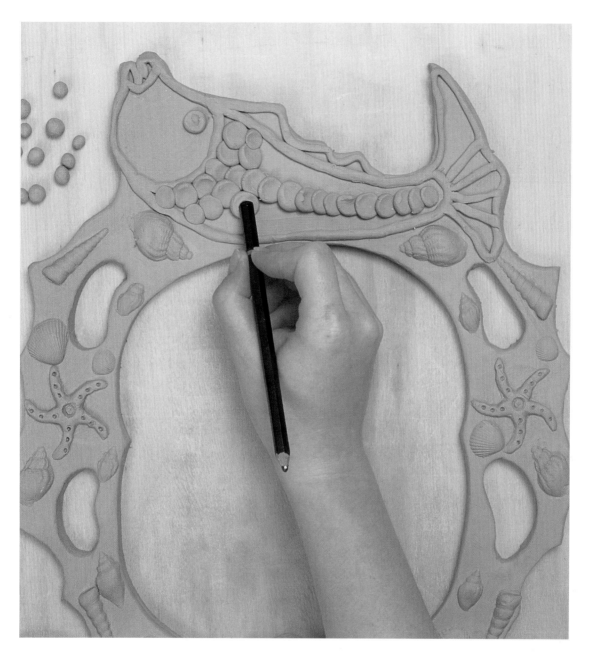

3 Define the outline of the fish with a series of small coils. To illustrate the scales of the fish, make a pile of small clay balls of varying sizes. Build the texture of the scales by pushing the balls into place with the end of a pencil. Use larger balls towards the head of the fish and smaller ones as you reach the tail. Leave until leather hard then clean up the back and the edges of the frame with a kitchen scourer. Bisque fire to 1120° C (2048° F).

FISH MIRROR

4 When you have retrieved the frame from the kiln, brush away any loose dust and apply the brush-on glazes. Paint on the blue first and then the green for the highlights. Ensure that you wipe the back of the mirror with a damp sponge to remove any excess glaze, then glaze fire to 1060° C (1940° F).

66

5 Using the template drawn in step 1, draw a line about 12 mm (½ in) in from the edge of the template all the way around, leaving a gap of 25 mm (1 in) at the top to allow the fixing of the D ring at a later stage. Take the template to a glass shop and ask them to cut a piece of 3 mm (⅛ in) thick mirror glass to fit inside the line.

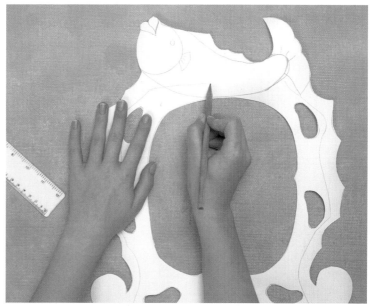

6 Using the credit card, spread some tile cement around the outer edge of the mirror on the reflecting side, take care as the edges of the mirror are extremely sharp. I recommend that you use gloves to protect against accidents at this stage. Press the mirror into place on the reverse of the frame. Some of the cement will ooze out from under the mirror so, still using the credit card, spread the excess cement back over the sharp edge then immediately clean off any excess from the front of the frame with a damp sponge. Leave until the tile cement has dried completely. Then clean using a scourer and some water to remove any traces of cement from the face of the mirror and frame, taking care not to scratch the mirror surface.

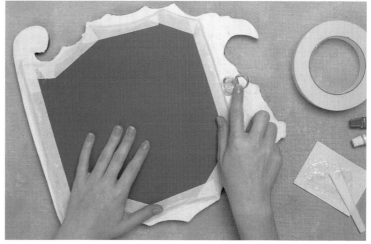

7 At this stage you can tape over the edge of the mirror with masking tape to cover any sharp edges. Using some epoxy resin, glue a D ring to the back of the frame. Leave to dry according to the manufacturer's instructions. You can cover the back of the mirror with felt. This can be glued directly on to the back of the frame.

SUNFLOWER VASE

SALLY JONES

This project has been devised for those new to pottery who do not have access to a kiln and have little experience with the medium of clay. There are several recently developed materials available that respond in a similar manner to clay which are able to take some forms of painted decoration. These materials have their limitations; however, for a beginner they are ideal as they dry quickly without cracking, retain their shape and have a robust dry strength with little or no brittle tendencies. The clay can be fired if required but this is not necessary.

To test the theory that this project could in fact be done by a beginner, I asked my sister Sally if she would undertake it. Sally has some design training but very little experience of ceramics. She found this project fun and easy to do.

Choose a vase that has an appealing shape, making sure it is not narrower at the top than the base and that it has no undercuts. The vase used here as a model is an ideal shape as it allows the new vase to just fall away from the original.

~

MATERIALS AND EQUIPMENT

● *vase* ● *paper* ● *sticky tape*
● *scissors* ● *nylon modelling*
clay (Newclay) ● *rolling pin*
● *rolling guides* ● *hessian*
cloth ● *bowl* ● *sponge*
● *craft knife* ● *potter's knife*
● *metal kidney* ● *stiff card*
● *pencil* ● *opaque stains in*
turquoise, yellow, orange and
green ● *soft, medium*
paintbrush ● *stencil brush*
● *matt spray sealer*

. . . . . .

1 Cover your chosen vase model completely in paper. Stick the paper in place with masking tape. Roll out a slab of modelling clay, then wrap this slab around the vase and cut to fit with a potter's knife; smooth the seam with a metal kidney. Add a further disc-shaped slab to form the base. Allow the clay to firm up a little and gently ease out your model vase from the inside. Do not allow the clay to get too dry as shrinkage will make it very difficult to remove the model. Allow the clay to firm until leather hard then smooth inside and out with a metal kidney, paying special attention to the base which needs to be level. Sponge sparingly to prevent the nylon fibres within the clay from being exposed. Leave aside until bone dry.

2 Use the paintbrush to paint the background colour, here a pale turquoise. If you wish, you can use ordinary acrylic paints for this job. Paint the inside as well as the outside of the vase and allow to dry completely.

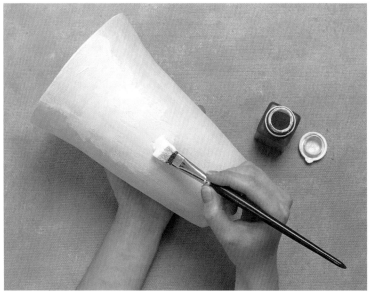

3 Cut a stencil from some card and position in place on the wall of the vase and hold it in place with your fingers. Apply your chosen colours to make up the tones of the flower, laying on the darker tones first. This will prevent further layers of colour obscuring each other. Build up the tones by using a fairly dry brush and stipple the colours sparingly. Allow the paint to dry between colours.

4 Spray with matt sealer inside and out. Your vase is now ready to be displayed with an imaginative display of dried flowers. Should you wish to place fresh flowers in your vase, all you need to do is to find a glass or other waterproof container that will fit inside.

NEPTUNE PEDESTAL BOWL

LIZA GARDNER

ADDING A PEDESTAL BASE is an attractive way of transforming a simple bowl into an effective centrepiece for a dinner table when filled with fruit and flowers. This shape of bowl can be used to serve your favourite seafood dish or will look equally spectacular in the bathroom filled with pot pourri or scented soaps.

The bowl is glazed with vibrant earthenware glazes in deep blues and greens, giving the piece a strong feeling of the ocean. The sea and its creatures have been a continual source of inspiration to artists for centuries and one to which I have been drawn since my days at art school.

~

MATERIALS AND EQUIPMENT

- *white earthenware clay*
- *kitchen scourer* • *old credit card* • *toothbrush*
- *knife* • *metal kidney*
- *cloth* • *rolling pin* • *rolling guides* • *bowl* • *sponge*
- *plaster bowl mould*
- *plaster mould of found objects (see page 30)* • *kiln*
- *spray gun and compressor*
- *lead-free earthenware clear glaze* • *copper and cobalt oxides* • *rutile*

. . . . . .

1 Roll out some clay on hessian cloth between two rolling guides to form a slab about 5 mm (¼ in) thick, and about 60 cm (25 in) square. It is not important to have straight or even edges at this stage. Place the slab of clay over the mould and gently lower it. As the clay starts to take the internal shape of the mould, push it into place with a gentle smoothing action. Take extreme care at this stage as the clay is fragile and can tear or crack if you rush. Press fully into the base of the mould and around the side walls with a wet sponge.

2 Smooth off the overhanging section that will form the rim of your bowl with the old credit card, making sure the rim is perfectly flat. The excess clay on this section can now be cut with a knife to create an even rim.

3 Roll small coils into the found object moulds to form your sprigging pieces. Scrape off any excess with the plastic card leaving the surface smooth and level. Use a small ball of clay to remove each of the sprigs from the moulds.

4 Position the sprigs on the rim of the bowl using your artistic judgement for a pleasing design. Once you have decided on the placing of the sprigs, gently mark the rim with a pencil to outline the positions. Remove the sprigs and lay them to one side. Score the surface of the rim inside the pencil outlines, cross hatching with a craft knife and slurrying the scored areas with a wet toothbrush.

5 Reposition the sprigged motifs on the rim and press down firmly, being careful not to damage the detailing. Leave to firm up until leather hard.

6 Remove the bowl from the mould, which should just drop out if it is dry enough. Turn upside-down on to a dry cloth, taking care not to damage the sprigs. Score around the base as for the rim and damp down with a toothbrush. Roll out some coils about 12 mm (½ in) in diameter and place the first one on the base of the bowl.

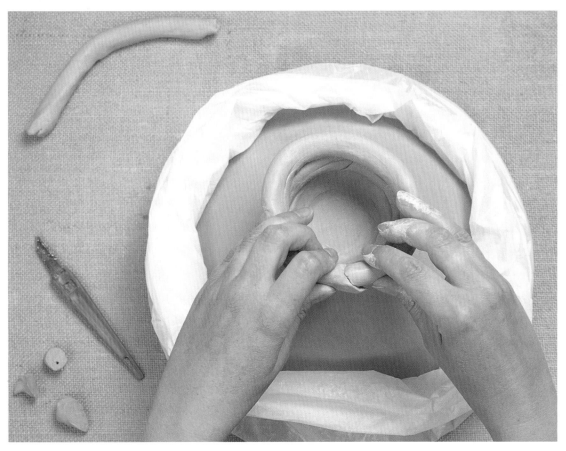

7 Using a metal kidney, smooth the coil on to the base and build up more coils until you reach about six coils high. Smooth the coils as you go along until you reach the desired height and shape. Leave the pot to firm up to leather hard and then scrape with a metal kidney to ensure that all the ridges and lumps have been smoothed out and that the base is level and flat. Finish off by lightly smoothing with a damp sponge.

Apply further sprigs to the dry surface. The principle is the same as before when applying sprigs to the rim of the bowl except that it is essential that the drying process is much slower. Make more sprig motifs and repeat the procedure in steps 3–5. Dry out slowly in a loosely draped plastic bag until the bowl is bone dry.

8 When fully dry, bisque fire to 1120° C (2048° F). When cool, brush out all particles of dust from around the sprigs then spray on the glaze making sure a good quality respirator is worn and that ventilation is adequate. Spray cobalt all over the piece, applying a slightly thicker coat on the seahorses. Then clean out your spray gun scrupulously and spray on the copper. Finally, splash on some rutile. The glaze should be the consistency of single cream and should be layered to about 1 mm (⅙₆ in) thick. Excess glaze should be wiped from the rim of the foot using a damp sponge and then the piece should be glaze fired at 1060–1080° C (1940–1976° F).

INLAID TILES

CHLOE GARDNER

This design is a four-tile repeat pattern with a border influenced by 17th-century Dervish-Tekke wall tiles from the 16th-century Palace of Ismail Bay. The construction technique is similar to that used in Victorian encaustic tile manufacture.

For beginners, it is probably best to experiment with a simple geometric design, and as your skill level increases, more complex designs can be attempted.

These tiles can be mounted and hung on the wall, or you could make a pot stand. The tiling of a complete kitchen worktop, including a space for a sink, should not be beyond the talents of most, and tiles are something that can be worked on over a period of time, say four tiles a week, until a whole worktop is completed.

~

MATERIALS AND EQUIPMENT

- white earthenware clay
- coloured body stains in cobalt, copper and canary yellow ● 80 mesh sieve
- 2 x wooden batts ● hessian cloth ● rolling pin and guides
- bowl ● sponge ● tracing paper ● pencil ● wire modelling tools (three basic shapes) ● craft knife
- potter's knife ● toothbrush
- metal scraper ● potter's needle ● kitchen scourer
- distilled vinegar
- paintbrush ● brush-on transparent glaze ● glaze mop ● tile cement ● grout
. . . . . .

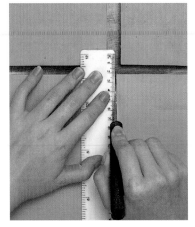

1 You will need to mix some coloured clays and the method for doing this is the same as mixing slip in step 1 on page 90, except that you will need to allow the mixture to dry to a plastic consistency and then it will need to be thoroughly wedged. Set aside and cover with a plastic bag. Roll out a slab of clay to about 8 mm (⅜ in) thick. Leave until leather hard. Measure and cut the tiles to the required size using a potter's or craft knife.

2 Trace the pattern or design using a soft pencil. Turn over the tracing paper, lay it on to the clay and gently press over the design with a blunt pencil which will leave a print on the clay. If you score a number on the back of the tiles at this stage it will make repositioning them in the correct order later much easier.

3 Cut the outline of your design with a potter's needle, go slowly on the corners! Carve out between the lines using modelling tools. When cutting out the design of the tile, carve out about one third of the tile's thickness. When finished, brush out the channels with a dry toothbrush to remove loose clay.

4 Roll out fine coils of coloured clay that you prepared earlier and fill in the channels, making your inserts a little proud of the tile surface. Leave the coloured clay to dry but not so much as to become leather hard. (Depending on room temperature this could be from 15 minutes to an hour.)

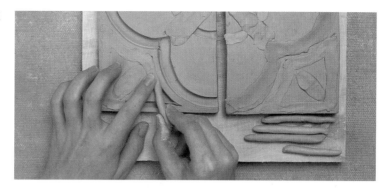

5 Scrape and smooth over the coloured clay with a steel scraper so that it is flush with the tile. Take care to ensure that the coloured clay doesn't smear over the main body of the tile. Where possible, scrape with the line of the pattern and this will reduce the chances of any smearing. Continue until you have crisp lines of pattern.

6 Dry out the tiles slowly, if you keep them loosely wrapped in polythene, this will largely prevent cracking. When the tiles are almost bone dry, clean up the edges with a kitchen scourer and brush away any loose dust. At this stage, there is a possibility that the different coloured clays will have shrunk at differing rates, leaving small gaps between the joins. If this is the case, apply some distilled vinegar to the cracks with a moderately stiff paintbrush; this will help to repair any cracks. Turn the tiles face down and sandwich them between two wooden batts to prevent warping. Leave until bone dry. Bisque fire to 1120°C (2048° F). When cool, remove the tiles from the kiln and brush on a clear mid-temperature transparent glaze and re-fire to 1060°C (1940° F).

WALL FOUNTAIN

LIZA GARDNER

This project is possibly the most ambitious in the book. Having said that, it can be undertaken by anyone who is willing to take time to plan their work and take things slowly. A prime consideration will be the size of the kiln you have available, as this may well limit the size of your fountain. The fountain has to be fired on its back so you should measure the inside of the kiln, allowing a gap of about 2.5 cm (1 in) all around the fountain for air circulation.

You will need to buy a small electric pump. In the photograph opposite you will notice a lump at the base of the fountain. This is the pump housing and its interior size is, of course, determined by the size of the pump. Many small, submersible pumps are available for pond fountains and are easy to fit if you follow the manufacturer's instructions. You will also need to find some small diameter plastic hose; this is usually sold in hardware stores.

⌣

MATERIALS AND EQUIPMENT

- *red terracotta clay* • *rolling pin* • *rolling guides*
- *wooden batt* • *hessian cloth*
- *bowl* • *sponge* • *craft knife*
- *potter's knife* • *toothbrush*
- *large rectangular metal kidney* • *serrated kidney*
- *card for template* • *pencil*
- *plaster mould for basin and pump housing* • *potter's large hole cutter* • *wire modelling tool* • *kiln* • *small electric submersible water pump*
- *plastic tubing*

. . . . . .

1 Roll out a slab of clay large enough for the full size of the fountain between the rolling guides and lay on a wooden batt. Place the pre-cut card template on top of the clay and cut out the basic shape with a craft knife.

2 Now cast two moulds, one as measured above for the pump housing and a larger one which is a half bowl shape to contain the water (see pages 30–33 on casting.) Make the originals from either coiled clay or a mass of clay which you can smooth to the shape required. Fill the half bowl-shaped mould with clay, cutting off any overhangs. Cover with plastic and lay aside. Fill the pump housing mould with clay, take off the plastic covers from the slab and bowl and allow to firm up until leather hard.

Smooth the surface with a large rectangular metal kidney. Smooth around the edges of the slab with a damp sponge. Place the water pump over the pump housing and measure the pump's width and height including the bend of the plastic hose without crushing it. This will determine the size of mould you will need to cast to completely house the water pump. Remember that clay shrinks approximately 10 per cent, so allow for this shrinkage when calculating the size required. It is a good idea to mark a centre line from the top to the bottom of your slab at this stage. Cover the slab with plastic and lay aside.

3 Place the pump housing against the half bowl and, using a potter's knife, score around the outside and the inner shape of the housing. This will leave two parallel lines marked on the bowl. Now cut away the inner line marked on the bowl. Then, using the serrated kidney, score between the remaining line and the cut you have just made.

4 Score the edge of the pump housing where it will join the bowl with a serrated kidney, slurry with a toothbrush and join the two parts with a coil laid on the outside of the join. Smooth down with your fingers both inside and outside of the join.

5 Assemble the bowl and pump housing to the back slab using a toothbrush and three coils, one for each half of the basin and one for the inside of the pump housing, do the pump housing first and smooth down all three coils as before.

6 You will now need to cut out two small pieces of clay which serve the purpose of concealing the entry points of the water pipe and electric cable that powers the motor. These small shelves can be decorated with a sprigged design of your choice and are shown in the photograph on the left hand side. Using the large hole cutter, cut out a hole of sufficient size for the cable and the water pipe to pass together through the back. When the hole has been tested for size, allowing for 10 per cent shrinkage, slurry the two small concealing shelf pieces into place where the top rim meets the back plate.

7 Roll out two long rectangles of clay which will be laid over the edge of the back plate. Score and slurry the back of the two shapes, lay into position, carefully easing the clay around the curves. They should abut the small concealing shelves mentioned in step 6 and be cut to stop at the centre line at the top of the back plate. Smooth the piece with a metal kidney and finish off with a damp sponge.

8 Choose various motifs for sprigging. I have used acanthus leaves cast from an old piece of ormolu, some detailing from a door knob and an a 19th century escutcheon plate found in a junk shop. Once chosen and cast, fix the resulting sprigs as usual (see page 75). For the rope decoration, I have rolled out two coils and gently intertwined them around each other. Lightly roll them out and position them on the back plate slab and the face of the bowl in elegant swags. Do not place them too close to the edge of the fountain as they are very fragile and can easily be broken if handled. A large sprig on the front of the pump housing is effective and, if at all possible, the same motif should be used for the next step.

9 Measure down the centre line of the fountain and, using the large hole cutter, cut a hole for the water pipe. Once this hole has been cut you will have no further use for the centre line and it can be smoothed away with the rectangular metal kidney. Use an acanthus leaf sprig or an equivalent, slightly bent between your fingers to conceal this hole. The bending of this sprigged piece has to be of sufficient curvature to allow the free passage of the end of the plastic hose without it being visible from the front of the fountain.

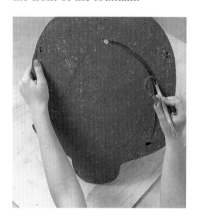

10 When the piece is firm, carefully lift it up and rest on the base of the pump housing. Turn the fountain so that you are looking at the rear of the back plate, then at the edges, about three-quarters of the way up, cut out two hanging recesses which should look like upside-down keyholes. Make these using the small hole cutter, then insert the head of a large screw into the circular hole and drag it upwards two or three times along the slot to create a dovetailed groove which will support the weight of the fountain when it is fixed to the wall. Cut away a groove with a wire modelling tool for the plastic pipe to pass from the pump housing to the upper hole, and a further groove from the pump housing to the side of the fountain which will allow the entry of the electric cable. It is very important to allow the fountain to dry out very slowly and thoroughly - at least four weeks. When fully dry, fire to 1120° C (2048° F).

Place the pump inside the housing and thread the electric cable and pipe through the hole in the back plate that you cut in step 6. Thread the plastic hose back through the hole in the top that was cut in step 9. The electric cable will have to be wired with a plug and connected to your supply, but do take care and if you at all unsure, consult an electrician. Fit the fountain to screws drilled into a wall by means of the two hanging recesses cut earlier, fill the bowl with water, switch on the electricity supply and watch the water flow.

WISTERIA PLATTER

LIZA GARDNER

COMMEMORATIVE PLATES were a reliable source of income for potters in medieval times, and slip trailing is the vibrant form of decoration common in this period. This decorative device often used geometric patterns framing figurative designs, script and numerals. Thomas Toft (working in the 1670s), is perhaps the most renowned of the practitioners of this branch of ceramics.

Bearing in mind the medieval origins of this form of decoration, I chose to explore medieval architecture. The stone carving on the columns of Chartres cathedral in France was the initial inspiration, large vines curling around the upper extremities of the columns with bunches of grapes festooned beneath the capitals. This exuberant and flowing design was then adapted to the platter shown here but instead of grape vines, I have used the wisteria that grows around the door of my studio.

~

MATERIALS AND EQUIPMENT

• plaster mould of an oval dish • white earthenware clay • coloured body stains in cobalt and copper • measuring scales • rolling pin • rolling guides • hessian cloth • bowl • sponge • knife • rubber kidney • slip trailer • pencil • glaze mop • brush- on lead-free transparent glaze

. . . . . .

1 You can buy slip ready mixed from most suppliers, or you can mix your own. The method is as follows: dry about 200 g (7 oz) of clay, the same type as you would normally use to make a platter or a bowl. Crush the dry clay in a bowl with the end of a rolling pin. Weigh out some pigment; if employing stains use approximately 15 per cent, if using oxides you will only need 3-5 per cent. Add to the clay and mix well. Add sufficient water to cover the mixture and leave to stand for 12 hours to allow the clay to dissolve completely. Thoroughly mix the slip and pour into another bowl through a 80 mesh sieve. When finished the consistency should be similar to a thick cream.

2 Roll out a slab of clay and carefully place over the mould, pressing in with a wet sponge and smooth off with a rubber kidney. (See page 74). Allow to firm up until the surface is still damp, but not sticky. Lightly draw your design on to the platter with a blunt pencil to provide guidelines for you to follow with the slip trailer.

3 Remove the nozzle from the slip trailer and express the air. Suck up some of the slip and replace the nozzle. Gently squeeze the bulb to remove any air and invert the slip trailer. Apply an even pressure and track along your design. It is a good idea to practise a line or two until you are confident. Do one colour at a time. If the slip does blob or spurt over your design, don't worry, as you can wipe any mistakes off with a damp sponge. Use smooth movements without stopping midway along a line.

4 After the first colour has dried to a stage where it no longer looks wet, repeat the process with the next colour. The flowers are composed of lots of small dots, called pearls, to build up the body of a wisteria bloom. Leave to dry under plastic overnight.

5 Take the platter out of the mould and clean up the rim and underside with a damp sponge. Leave until bone dry.

6 Bisque fire to 1120° C (2048° F) and then glaze with a transparent brush-on glaze. If you wish, use a slight coloration by way of a stain or an oxide in your glaze to give a more vibrant lift to the platter, but do not use too much as this will obscure the colours of the slips.

PATTERNS

Four Fish Salad Bowl page 34

Use a photocopier to enlarge this
pattern by 165%

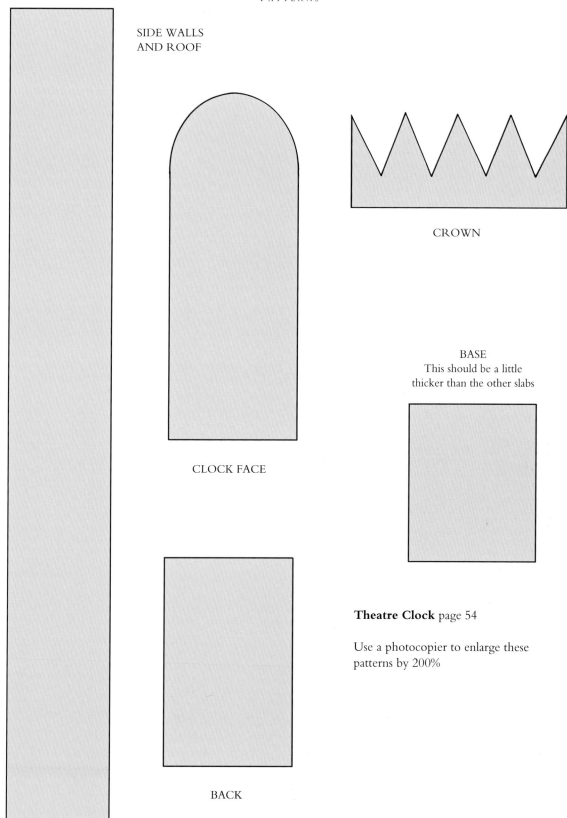

SIDE WALLS
AND ROOF

CROWN

CLOCK FACE

BASE
This should be a little
thicker than the other slabs

Theatre Clock page 54

Use a photocopier to enlarge these
patterns by 200%

BACK

SUPPLIERS

UNITED KINGDOM
BRICK HOUSE CRAFTS
Cock Green, Felsted, Essex CM6 3JE
Tel: 01371 820502 Fax: 01371 820975
(Suppliers of every material that the potter requires.)

THE CROMARTIE GROUP
Park Hall Road, Longton,
Stoke-on-Trent ST3 5AY
Tel: 01782 313947
(Supply kilns and wheels, etc.)

DEANCRAFT LTD
Suite 3 Enterprise Centre, Moorland Road,
Burslem, Stoke-on-Trent, Staffordshire ST6 1JQ
Tel: 01782 834580 Fax: 01782 834603
*(Suppliers of materials and tools. Also offer advisory and
mail-order service.)*

POTCLAYS LTD
Brickkiln Lane, Stoke-on-Trent ST4 7BP
Tel: 01782 286506
(Supply full range of materials.)

POTTERYCRAFTS
Cambell Road, Stoke-on-Trent, ST4 4ET
Tel: 01782 745000
(Supply full range of materials.)

SPECIALIST CRAFTS LTD
PO Box 247, Leicester, LE1 9QS
Tel: 0116 2510405
*(Supply full range of materials. Mail order service
available from comprehensive catalogue.)*

W. J. FURSE & CO LTD
Wilford Road, Nottingham, NG2 1EB
Tel: 0115 9863471
(Supply water pumps)

AUSTRALIA
CERAMIC AND CRAFT CENTRE
11 Green Street, Revesby 2212, NSW
Tel: 02 771 6166 Fax: 02 771 6011

CERAMIC AND CRAFT CENTRE
52 Wecker Road, Mansfield 3722, Queensland
Tel: 07 3343 7377 Fax: 07 349 5052

CERAMIC HOBBIES PTY LTD
12 Hanrahan Street, Thomastown 3074, Victoria
Tel: 03 4662522 Fax: 03 464 0547

CERAMICRAFT
33 Deeinup Way, Malaga 6062, Western Australia
Tel: 09 249 9266 Fax: 09 249 9690

CREATIVE SUPPLIES PTY LTD
Unit 10/2 Clare Mace Crescent,
Berkeley Vale 2506, NSW
Tel: 043 88 4560 Fax: 043 88 1521

THE PUG MILL PTY LTD
17a Rose Street, Mile End 5031, South Australia
Tel: 08 43 4544 Fax: 08 345 0991

NEW ZEALAND
ARUM PRODUCTS
142 Eastern Hutt Road, Taita, Wellington
Tel: 04 567 2688

CCG INDUSTRIES LTD
33 Crowhurst Street, Newmarket
Tel: 09 524 9758

NZ HOBBY CLAY & CRAFT CO LTD
1/180 James Fletcher Drive, Mangere
Tel: 09 270 0140

WESTERN POTTERS SUPPLIES
4/43 Lindwood Avenue, Mt Albert
Tel: 09 815 1513

Contributors' Studio addresses:
MARIA ALQUILAR
703 Darwin Street, Santa Cruz, CA 95062, USA
Tel: 408 423 2490

JESSICA BALL
Unit 2a, Thomas James Centre, Bridge House
Lane, Haworth, West Yorkshire B22 8PA, England
Tel: 01535 647221

LIZA GARDNER CERAMICS
Adorno's Hut, 96c Bedford Hill, London
SW12 9HR, England
Tel: 0181 673 2022/1946

GILLIAN HODGE
11009 Spenceville Road, Penn Valley,
CA 95946, USA
Tel: 916 432 1512

JEFF IRWIN
1760 W Arbor Dr, San Diego, CA 92103, USA
Tel: 619 294 4075

SUSIE LEAR
45a Langroyd Road, London SW17 7PL, England
Tel: 0171 720 9919

GENEVIEVE NIELSON
The Gallery, 13 Victoria Street, Englefield Green,
Surrey TW20 0QU, England
Tel: 01784 430516

RIMMINGTON★VIAN
Phillip Rimmington or Kevin Vian, 5a Illife Yard,
London SE17 3QA, England
Tel: 0171 708 0864

SARAH PERRY
55 Annandale Road, London SE10 0DE, England
Tel/fax 0181 858 2663

BARBARA SEBASTIAN
1777 Yosemite Avenue, San Francisco,
CA 94124, USA
Tel: 415 822 3243

LAURANCE SIMON
Westland Studios, 3-11 Westland Place,
London N1 7LP, England
Tel: 0171 250 3224

FURTHER READING
HISTORICAL
Burton Anthony, *Josiah Wedgwood: A Biography*,
Andre Deutsch, 1979

Charleston Robert J, (Ed.) *World Ceramics*,
Hamlyn, 1981 (Softback ed.)

Hamilton David, *Manual of Pottery & Ceramics*,
Thames & Hudson, 1974

Jervis Simon, *The Penguin Dictionary of Design &
Designers*, Penguin, 1984

Lane Arthur, *Style in Pottery*, Faber & Faber, 1973

Pevsner Nikolaus, *Pioneers of Modern Design*,
Penguin, 1991

Wills Geoffrey, *Wedgwood*, Pyramid, 1989

GENERAL
Clark Kenneth, *Pottery Throwing for Beginners*,
Studio Vista, 1970

Lane Peter, *Studio Ceramics*, Wm Collins, 1984

Leach Bernard, *A Potter's Book*, Faber & Faber,
1940

Wondrausch Mary, *On Slipware*, A&C Black, 1986

INDEX